ROGUES AND RASCALS

ROGUES AND RASCALS

True Stories of Maritime Lives and Legends

Bob Kroll

Nimbus Publishing Limited
3731 Mackintosh St, Halifax, NS B3K 5A5
(902) 455-4286 nimbus.ca

Printed and bound in Canada

FSC
www.fsc.org
MIX
Paper from responsible sources
FSC® C013916

Author photo: Mary Reardon
Design: Jenn Embree

Library and Archives Canada Cataloguing in Publication

Kroll, Robert E., 1947-
Rogues and rascals : true stories of Maritime lives and legends / Bob Kroll.
ISBN 978-1-55109-864-7

1. Maritime Provinces—Biography. 2. Maritime Provinces—History--Miscellanea. I. Title.

FC2029.K76 2011 971.5009'9 C2011-903912-5

NOVA SCOTIA
Communities, Culture and Heritage

Nimbus Publishing acknowledges the financial support for its publishing activities from the Government of Canada through the Canada Book Fund (CBF) and the Canada Council for the Arts, and from the Province of Nova Scotia through the Department of Communities, Culture and Heritage.

To Julia, Ellery, Sarah, Viola, Xavier, and Rebecca

CONTENTS

Preface

The people in these stories were real. The stories are true. Occasionally I fleshed out the historical bones with details from other sources. And sometimes I attributed motive to actions and coloured personal conduct with feelings.

Thirty years ago, I set out to find true stories about ordinary people in the Maritimes: stories about everyday life; stories about the odd, the interesting, and the unusual; and about misfits and malingerers, heroes and failures, hucksters, soul savers, and criminals. I sought stories about our ancestors and how they lived.

I discovered that people are people—past and present. Our motives and behaviours are not a whole lot different from those of our forefathers. And I came to realize that history is a harmony of the deeds and misdeeds of people, a seamless pattern of random and sometimes discordant sounds that somehow swirl together into a melody. Open this book anywhere, and imagine the two of us in a setting of your choice, telling stories about our ancestors—warts and all.

The historical sources for these stories include Nova Scotia, New Brunswick, and Prince Edward Island Supreme Court cases and judgement books, Courts of General Quarter Sessions cases, coroners' reports, grand jury books, official government correspondence, and Executive Council minutes, as well as various family papers, letters, and diaries. Newspapers were an excellent source for detailing criminal activities and the deeds of community-favourite sons and daughters, as well as odd, interesting, and unusual happenings throughout the region. Secondary sources played an important role as well, such as *Tales of Abegweit, Loyalists of Shelburne, Lifeline, Shipwrecks of Nova Scotia, Pioneer Profiles of New Brunswick Settlers, Rambles Among the Bluenoses, The Old Attorney General,* and others. Secondary sources also include numerous scrapbooks (held in provincial archives) containing time-tinted newspaper articles, personal recollections, and photos.

Heidi MacDonald helped with the Prince Edward Island side of the research, and B. J. Grant helped with New Brunswick. At the time, Heidi was a graduate student at the University of New Brunswick.

Barry John Grant was a New Brunswick author. He often wrote his research into stories, and, when he did, I hardly changed a word. I identified his contributions with his initials—BJG.

Bob Kroll
April 30, 2011

Old Comers and New Comers

A POWERFUL PREACHER

In 1823, two strangers arrived in Halifax on the packet boat from Saint John, New Brunswick. The man was nothing but skin and bone, and his wife a puny waste of womanhood. Their wretched appearance caught the town's attention. Merchants and tradesmen kept a close eye on this ragtag couple, who took a cellar room on the waterfront.

About a week later, this man, who called himself Jackson, rented McIntyre's Hall on Gottingen Street, behind St. George's Round Church. He announced in the newspaper that he would preach the word of God to both sinners and saved.

That night, McIntyre's Hall bulged with a mix of sinners, scorners, and those throbbing with curiosity. Jackson took the makeshift pulpit. His voice was a lullaby one moment, a thunderbolt the next.

He told of arriving in Halifax bent and hungry, and how each night he prayed and prayed for sustenance with what little strength he had left. Then one morning, he woke to find on his doorstep a barrel of mackerel and another of flour. A gift from God, he proclaimed. A miracle! "And here I stand before you, proud and healthy, living proof of God's mercy."

The next day, throughout Halifax, it was "Jackson said this" and "Jackson said that." His congregation swelled immediately, and within a month, Jackson had his own revivalist church on Brunswick Street.

People must have been hungry to hear a powerful preacher, for they travelled from miles around by foot, buggy, and ox cart to listen to the glory of Jackson's voice.

But a preacher's voice is seldom enough to hold a congregation for long. Within a few months, there was dissent among the ranks. Some wanted Jackson to preach more fire and brimstone, and others wanted less. Some wanted religious ritual, while others preferred only words.

One Sunday, the deacon was returning up the aisle with the collection basket brimming with hard cash. A man sitting on the aisle made an insulting remark about Jackson's sermon, something about it deserving little more than a halfpenny for its ability to stir the soul.

The deacon stopped suddenly and brought the collection basket down on the man's head. Coins flew everywhere, and the congregation dived after them. Many of the less devout pocketed what they grabbed, and shoved aside others in order to gather more. A fight broke out. Women screamed. Families fled.

Needless to say, there was no benediction at that service. And within the month, Jackson and wife boarded a coaster boat bound for Boston.

FOSS'S DAM

(BJG)

Charles Orrin Foss hit New Brunswick in 1921. He was a Yankee by birth, a civil engineer by trade, and a very persuasive man. He was so persuasive that he convinced New Brunswick's premier, Walter Foster, to finance the idea of generating the province's electricity and selling it. He also persuaded the premier's daughter to marry him.

When Foster's government decided to go into the electricity-making business, it dammed the Musquash River, a considerable stream that flows into the Bay of Fundy a few miles west of Saint John..

The dam was fairly finished in 1923 when the province was hit by one of the worst series of floods ever. Up and up the water behind the Musquash dam rose, until the whole top of it became a spillway. The centre of Foss's dam held, but pressure punched holes near each bank. It seems somebody, in order to save money and pay a kickback, forced the contractors to use mainly loose gravel instead of good sand, and also shortchange on the amount of cement.

No one witnessed the disaster, but at ten o'clock on the night of April 30, 1923, the enormous roar carried for miles as most of Foss's dam went raging down the stream bed. Only the greater lumps of concrete remained. And the raging waters created a kind of new inland delta of red mud.

One human life was lost: a farmer drowned while trying to save a cow from the reddish mire. And Foss's career was ruined. Leaving all behind, including his wife and family, Foss bought a railway ticket and disappeared. The only thing of him that ever returned to New Brunswick was his obituary—two years later. Charles Orrin Foss had died in California.

ELIJAH ROOP

The Roop brothers, Elijah and John, had settled land in Nova Scotia where a half-dozen underground springs bubbled to the surface with the promise that the soil here was as good as it gets. The land was in the south woods fifty miles from nowhere, and the place was called "Grinton's Settlement." Many years later, another group of people would change the name to "Springfield," which they thought better described the place where water bubbled from the ground. These newcomers thought "Grinton's Settlement" said little about the place, except that John Grinton had settled here first. And he had, in 1819.

John Grinton was the first to follow the grown-over military trail from Lawrencetown and stake his claim at one of those bubbling springs. The Roop brothers were close to follow behind. The Roops were New York Dutch, and the boys were of second-generation Loyalist stock. Their parents had run from the American Revolution to settle at Granville Ferry, near Annapolis Royal. The boys were twins, orphaned when they were twelve, homesteading when they were fifteen.

The brothers learned of government land grants along the old military road, near where the Grintons, the McNairs, and the Stoddards had settled. The Nova Scotia government wanted to fill up the interior of the colony with dirt farmers and cattlemen who would feed Halifax and most of the colony's coastal communities.

At first the government had given interior land to a ragtag bunch of disbanded soldiers from Halifax. But soldiers were better at fighting than they were at farming. They were good at drinking too, and trading their land and government provisions for whatever rotgut drink would quench their thirst. So the government gave up on soldiers as settlers, and opened up the south woods of Nova Scotia to anyone willing to stake a claim, clear trees, and cultivate a living off ground that John Grinton and Boyd McNair said was as rich as any thereabouts.

The Roop brothers loaded their backs with grub and tools, and walked more than a hundred miles over a path tangled with underbrush and scrub trees. They walked their feet swollen until they reached the "Fingerboard," a road sign near Albany Cross that pointed the way they wanted to go. Then they walked to a hill overlooking a lake (now Springfield Lake) that held the sky like a mirror. It was as though the brothers shared the same dream of a homestead, a fire-and-ice vision of side-by-side living and dying at a place where the maple and birch raised colour in the wind, and the dark furrows of a newly ploughed field ran the arc of the lake that made two of everything. No sooner had they broken from the dark foliage of the tree line, than the twins dropped the supplies they carried, grabbed axes, and started clearing.

They felled trees with the endless energy of youth, burning slash, bucking logs for building, and sawing up branches for heating the home they would share. Every day for four weeks they cut and chopped during every waking moment, until the night closed over them and sleep took a mallet to their heads.

Then one hot day, after a morning of hard clearing, John Roop straightened up from chopping a large pine. His face was the colour of wet plaster. The axe fell from his hands and he grabbed his chest. He stumbled among the tree fall to where his brother was chopping and fell into a heap of slash, boughs, and wood chips.

Elijah loaded his brother onto his shoulders and lugged him over that stony path toward Lawrencetown; lugged him two miles, maybe three, with every step feeling a hurt like no hurt he had ever felt, feeling as though he was carrying one-half of his own self. Then

Elijah weakened under the awful burden of truth and lowered his brother onto a bed of pine needles and saw what he had known since before he set out: John was dead.

Elijah buried John on the hill overlooking the lake and marked the grave with a cairn of stones. In time, the grave became a graveyard, a fenced-in plot, the whole of it framed by the cabin window where on most nights Elijah sat and watched, warming himself at the fire. He never got used to winter, not even after Annie Felch married him in 1827 and bore him two live sons, Major and Charles. There were other children, stillborn in the birch bed he had made before the wedding. He buried them in that graveyard—dug the graves himself, and marked them with three slate stones that stood beside his brother's cairn. Elijah mourned the losses most days of his life. In good weather, he would visit the family plot. And when the weather turned cold, he would sit at the cabin window and watch leaves, and later, snow, pile on the graves, feeling the cold brood of death in that winter.

TURNBULL'S WAR

At twenty-two years of age, John Turnbull left Charlottetown, Prince Edward Island, for Boston and joined the U.S. navy as a foreign national. He served as a coal heaver on board the USS *Baltimore*, a warship—the biggest and best-equipped warship of its day. In the spring of 1891, the *Baltimore* sailed for Chile to protect American interests there during a full-blown revolution. The ship arrived at Valparaiso and almost at once seemed to anger both sides just by being there.

After six months, the revolution quieted; or so it seemed to Captain Sheeley, who had granted the sailors of the USS *Baltimore* liberty. Bill Turnbull was one of the 117 sailors to go ashore. They ran smack-dab into a gang of Chilean toughs in an angry mood, their passion still horned up from the violence of the revolution. It was more a brawl than a battle, and most of the sailors managed to make their way back to the ship uninjured.

Bill Turnbull was in a bar when the fighting broke out. Bill had his back to the door when a man named Carlos Gomez rushed in and stabbed him from behind. Turnbull staggered into the street, and then the mob took over. They stabbed Bill Turnbull eighteen times with knives and bayonets, and left him on the street to die.

President Benjamin Harrison and the U.S. Congress were outraged. They rattled their sabres and called for a declaration of war. The Chilean government issued a formal apology to avoid war with the U.S., and paid out seventy-five thousand dollars to atone for the attack on the sailors and the brutal murder of Bill Turnbull.

On October 27, 1891, the U.S. government buried Bill Turnbull from Charlottetown, PEI, with full military honours in a Valparasio cemetery. They marked his grave with a fine tombstone; and in the annals of U.S. history, they called this incident "Turnbull's War."

COUNTRY BOY

Frank Jones was from Stanley Bridge, up along the Nashwaak River in New Brunswick. He was a country boy right to the bone, and in 1899, he made up his mind to get a taste of the big city—Saint John.

Frank was in Saint John hardly two hours when he met the love of his life, a painted-faced woman named Phoebe Dukshire. Phoebe was about ten years older than Frank, and she knew her way around. She offered to show Frank what she knew, but it would cost him a few coins from the money purse he carried. It seemed Phoebe had a price for every moment she spent with Frank and for everything they did together. They walked along the waterfront and throughout the city. That cost Frank a dollar. They sat on a bench and Frank gabbed about country life, about fishing and hunting and the freedom of living in the outdoors. That cost a dollar more. That night, Phoebe took Frank home. It was a busy place, a sort of boarding house to Frank's mind, with a lot of comings and goings. The price doubled.

On October 7, two police officers, McFadden and Amos, raided a house on Sheffield Street. This house was well known to the Saint John police, as well as to every sailor who landed in Saint John.

McFadden and Amos dragged from the house about half a dozen women in various stages of undress and an equal number of men. One of the prisoners was Phoebe Dukshire. Another was Frank Jones.

The next day, Frank stood before a magistrate, charged with being an inmate of a disorderly house. Frank innocently said he wasn't. He said he was seeing a girl named Phoebe. Frank figured a night with Phoebe meant they were engaged, because he told the judge he was fixing to marry her.

The judge took pity on this country boy. He told Frank Jones to go back to Stanley Bridge at once if he wanted to escape a year's imprisonment. That was good advice, and Frank took it!

By the way, Phoebe got a one-hundred-dollar fine and six months in jail.

HARRIETSFIELD DUEL

Christian Werner lived in Harrietsfield, Nova Scotia, a stony patch of ground on the outskirts of Halifax. Werner was a German settler who owned a mangy dog that had a habit of wandering onto William Thompson's property and chasing Thompson's sheep.

Thompson never had much to do with Christian Werner. Thompson spoke no German, and Werner's English was none too good. Thompson was also the local Justice of the Peace, and Werner a hard-luck dirt farmer.

In June 1796, Werner's dog again chased Thompson's sheep. This time, Thompson stomped over to Werner's place with a loaded musket. The German was out in a back field. Thompson cornered the dog, levelled his musket, and shot the dog dead.

Werner's wife saw the whole affair. That night, Werner, fuming over his dead dog, put quill to paper and challenged Thompson to a duel the following morning. A hired hand delivered the challenge to Thompson.

Thompson puzzled over the note, then shook his head in confusion. He knew it was from Werner, but he had no idea what it said. Werner had written the challenge in German.

The following morning, Thompson was a no-show for the duel. Furious at not getting satisfaction, Werner wrote a second challenge. This one he delivered himself. To make sure Thompson got the message, Werner slapped Thompson on the cheek and openly challenged the Justice of the Peace to a duel.

Still not understanding a word Werner had written or said, Thompson went to his writing desk and wrote out a warrant for

Christian Werner's arrest. The charge was common assault. He wrote the charge in English; and the sheriff who served it understood every word.

MISFIT SAILORS

Joe Scaling and Art Spearing had fallen on hard times. It was the 1890s, and a good part of the world was suffering a deep economic depression. Scaling and Spearing were from Cambridge, Nova Scotia. Though neither had been to sea, they went down to the Halifax waterfront and begged one sea captain after another to take them on board.

Captain Harry Smith was from Cambridge, and his heart went out to these two hometown boys. He offered them a chance on board his ship, which was sailing for South America with a load of lumber.

Scaling and Spearing sent word to their wives that they were off to sea, and the following morning, they set sail.

Both were seasick the entire trip. But in their minds, that did not matter; for they had jobs, and no matter how sick they were, so long as they hauled and heaved, in that order, they would get paid.

Off Key West, they ran head-on into a fierce gale. The ship seemed to blow six ways at once, and Captain Harry had all he could do to keep her bow running with the waves. At one point, Captain Harry hollered to Joe Scaling, "Let go the spanker!"

Now, a spanker is a fore-and-aft sail, and Captain Harry wanted it released to help keep the ship's bow with the waves. But Joe Scaling misunderstood and hollered to Art Spearing, "Let go the anchor!"

Spearing did just that. The ship yawed from the anchor's weight and drag, and turned broadside to the next crushing wave. It required all of Captain Harry's skill to keep that ship afloat and bring her around.

When they reached port in South America, Captain Harry told Scaling and Spearing, "On the return trip, you're sailing as passengers, not crew!"

NOT A SHILLING MORE

On November 2, 1749, Lieutenant John Hamilton led a company of eighteen redcoat soldiers on patrol of the area surrounding Annapolis Royal. They were on the lookout for Acadian farmers trading food and munitions with the French military.

Hamilton later reported that he saw nothing but dense forest aflame in fall colours, and heard nothing but the clomp and clamber of his soldiers marching the narrow path. Then all at once the branches parted, and the trees took the shape of French soldiers and Mi'kmaq warriors.

Hamilton sized up the situation quickly. He figured he was outnumbered twenty to one. And showing more brains than guts, he surrendered without firing a shot.

The French and the Mi'kmaq rounded up the soldiers and transported them overland to Quebec City. Here, a couple of years later, Hamilton reported meeting other captives from Halifax—captives like Tom Standard, John Witherspoon, and Honora Hancock. There were sixty in all, most captured outside the Halifax palisade that protected the new settlement.

The French wanted a ransom for their return. The governor and Executive Council at Halifax agreed to pay, but it took more than two years to negotiate the deal. The final figure was sixty-six pounds per person, plus transportation costs.

How both sides calculated such a precise ransom is unknown. But one thing seems certain—government in the eighteenth century knew the value of each one of its citizens, and was willing to pay it, but not one shilling more.

BURRS AND WILDFLOWERS

Amy Williams was laced lamb and loose leather. She was a head-turning woman who had a smile of sunshine, a body of alabaster, and the morals of a barracks cat.

Amy was among the first settlers to land in Halifax, Nova Scotia, in June 1749. She had travelled with her husband, William, a lieutenant in His Majesty's army. During that long, seasick crossing, Amy had William crazy mad and storming the deck to defend her honour from several unmarried men who got their breeches tight whenever she sashayed on deck for a breath of salty air. Which was often. More often than her husband preferred. So often that William carried a charged pistol in his belt, a powder horn on his shoulder, and a ramrod ready for driving home a second load.

Hardly a day passed on board the transport ship that Amy did not flirt and William did not back down her lusty pursuers by wrapping his fingers around the handle of his gun. Sooner or later, one of these men was bound to stand up to William's threats, and

William knew it. Feared it. Wished to Jesus his wife would stop this flirting and not force him to empty a plug of jealousy into another man's heaving, beating heart.

But Amy did not stop. She did not even try. The truth is, the more William reined in her boldness, the bolder Amy behaved. About the only thing that kept William from hot-blooded murder, and hanging from the yardarm of the transport ship, was the sight of land.

Tree-covered land. Vast. Dangerous. Daring. Land that was a lot like Amy Williams—ripe and ready.

It was 1,400 slack-jawed, baggy-assed, and bone-faced settlers—mostly men—and a couple hundred soldiers who scraped that slope of land bald. They gouged a town into a mud-running hillside. They parcelled lots, and threw up log homes and clapboard shacks. By November, most held snug for the winter behind a palisade of sharpened poles.

Lieutenant William Williams drew a lot on the west side of Grafton Street, about three doors in from the corner at George. His two-room cabin was cozy by any standards, yet his wife preferred the dark snuggle she found at Shippey's Tavern on the waterfront. Sailors drank there. Soldiers, too. Shippey's was a dim knot of rough talk, shadows, and lewd behaviour. Twice Lieutenant Williams had to draw his pistol to get her out of there, and twice Amy clawed his face and arms to stay.

One day in January 1750, Amy got the bright idea to start selling what she had been giving away. She applied for and was granted her own license to sell liquor, and within a month, the Williamses' front door was a turnstile to Amy's affections and personal favours. Officers came and went day and night. Drunk. Eager. Waiting their turn with the woman who was back-scratch wild in bed. Each believed Amy was his and his alone, and each snapped silver on a dresser table before he left. In the barracks, they argued among themselves. There were fist fights. Duels. Some shirked their duty by lolling lob-legged in their bunks, sore and twisting with desire for Amy Williams.

Word spread throughout the town—Amy Williams was trouble. More trouble than the town needed, with the French rattling their sabres in Fortress Louisbourg, and the Mi'kmaq across the harbour, threatening with their tomahawks. Even the governor and his Executive Council heard all about Amy Williams, and about her den of sin on Grafton Street.

Governor Edward Cornwallis described Amy in a letter to the Lords of Trade in England as "a wretched woman whose conduct was infamous." Malachi Salter, a merchant and a member of the Executive Council, was more discreet. He simply said Amy had let out her front room more often than an innkeeper's wife.

Lieutenant William Williams preferred living in the barracks to going home. It was painful enough to hear the tavern talk about his wife without having to see another man harden to her affections.

Then one night Lieutenant Williams got himself stumble drunk, and long and longing for the woman he loved. His heart was a scab itching for the scratch of seeing her. Williams never bothered knocking on his own door. He just threw the latch and saw his wife's woozy face puckered for love. He saw Amy and Captain Thomas buff naked and lying on the floorboards.

Hurt sometimes squeezes a mind that is blurry of reason and coats the nerves insensitive, so that a man with a pistol in his belt does in an instant what his brain would otherwise tell him not to do. Sometimes, however, hurt has the opposite effect. Sometimes hurt sharpens the edge on one's thinking and cuts through the confusion of raw emotion, to allow one to do something precise and controlled—like smiling broadly, and setting the time and location for a face-up, twelve-pace, balled-back duel.

Lieutenant Williams and Captain Thomas met outside the south gate of the palisade, behind the place where the town had marked off a burying ground. There was nothing romantic about the encounter. No misty morning sunrise. No bird-chirping, cricket-scratching silence. It was just a dreary, egg-white day during the January thaw, with the sound of horse-beaten mud sucking at five pairs of boots—the duellists, two seconds, and a witness.

The seconds measured off twelve paces, then informed Williams and Thomas that neither should take aim. The duellists should simply raise their pistols and fire. Williams stood with his back to a white birch. He chewed his lips and shifted his weight uneasily. Thomas stumbled to a position beside a tree stump. He fidgeted with the loose braid on his red tunic. His second had to place the pistol in his hand and guide his finger over the trigger.

Williams raised his pistol and fired. The blast brought a squeal from Thomas, whose own pistol went off and fired into the ground. Neither man was injured, yet in the lagging gun smoke, neither could see the cold, ash-coloured face of the other.

Thomas's second called for a reload, as though the stink of spent powder had quickened his thirst for blood. Williams refused. He shoved his pistol into his belt and walked away, his chin down, his shoulders rolled forward, his spirit beaten raw to a blister.

Later that day, Lieutenant William Williams applied for a divorce, and a few weeks later, Governor Edward Cornwallis granted it. The governor, too, had had enough of this woman who in seven months of settlement had driven nearly a dozen of his officers fighting mad with lust. With the full agreement of his Executive Council, and well within his authority as a colonial governor, Cornwallis ordered Amy Williams to catch the spring packet boat out of Nova Scotia.

On May 15, 1750, Lieutenant William Williams slogged through the muddy streets to the waterfront. When Williams reached the dock, the packet boat for Boston was gone on yesterday's tide, a sailor said, and the woman too. Gone with it. Gone double in the captain's bunk.

Williams glumly retreated along the dock. He drank himself stupid that night, and repeated over and over to anyone who would listen that it was all just burrs and wildflowers, burrs and wildflowers. That's all love was. Burrs and wildflowers and chimney smoke.

EARLY JAILS

New Englanders proudly point to the hardiness of their first settlers, noting their seventeenth-century Puritan values and nose-to-the-grindstone work ethic as reasons for the early success of their colonies. Nova Scotia can make no such lofty claim. Halifax's first settlers were unskilled pioneers swept from England's slums, poor houses, and upland hovels. They preferred royal handouts to hard work, and the flagon to the axe.

According to Governor Edward Cornwallis, these settlers hit the beach in 1749 expecting to get something for nothing. Governor Cornwallis described only 300 of the 1,400 settlers as industrious:

"The rest are poor, idle, worthless vagabonds that embraced the opportunity to get provisions for one year without labour."

Cornwallis was referring to the settlers who lived off a sort of government grant. But there were others who had more devious ways to make a living "without labour."

Mary Ann Hollwell was one. After wading ashore in 1749, she hardly waited for the hem of her dress to dry before she stole from Joshua Mauger and Isaac Deschamps one looking glass, three pairs of children's silk stockings, two knives, one leather dish, a bottle of lavender water, and three handkerchiefs. And that was just for starters. The following month, she sneaked into Richard Catherwood's dry goods store and took one half-piece of satin ribbon and a small china mug. Then she returned to Isaac Deschamps's store to help herself to a dress to match the satin ribbon she had pinched from Catherwood's.

She claimed she had purchased these items in Dublin before departing for Halifax, and she had two witnesses to back her up—Robert Benson and Abraham Rushworth. The judge did not buy Benson and Rushworth's testimony. He convicted Mary Ann of theft and sentenced her to thirty-nine stripes at the public whipping post.

Mary Ann would embrace that post a time or two more over the next three years. By 1752, Mary Ann Hollwell's naked back looked like an English countryside, with its checkered pattern of welts from the lash "well laid on."

Mary Ann was one of many. Joseph Moore was another. He stole a soldier's uniform simply to keep warm. And Robert Brown unpinned a handkerchief from John Faggin's wash line to trade for a gill of rum.

Joblessness and poverty gave motive for these settlers to filch what wasn't theirs. And a barter economy provided them with the opportunity to easily unload what they had stolen. The result was a crime wave of petty theft. In 1752, this moved Halifax justices of the peace to petition the governor and the Executive Council for a "Bridewell," a workhouse "...to which such offenders might be committed and there employed in hard labour..."

Those sent to the workhouse were "disorderly and idle persons, beggars, fortune tellers, gamblers, drunkards, vagabonds, persons of lewd behaviour, runaways, stubborn servants and children."

The Executive Council, the government of Nova Scotia at the time, expropriated the stone house of Richard Wenman to serve as the workhouse, and hired Wenman as jail keeper. Prisoners received ten lashes upon entering the jail, and during their term could be whipped at the jail keeper's discretion. Prisoners paid for their meals and liquor, as well as rent for their jail cells, which were small and cramped, cold, damp, bug-infested, and foul. Charles Donovan died in the Halifax jail because he could not afford the cost of food.

In 1759, Alice Wallace, a petty thief, petitioned the Nova Scotia Supreme Court for an immediate trial: "...because being so low, she is not able to live a winter in this miserable place."

On August 19, 1764, Governor Wilmot wrote to the Lords of Trade, almost bragging about how duties on rum had financed the building of a new workhouse in Halifax "...in which there is also a poor house, which houses the old, infirm, indigent, together with the dissolute and abandoned."

Prisoners had to pay the jail keeper for his services, and those not having the means to pay had to rely on public charity for their food, clothes, and bedding. In 1818, George Robertson, the current jail keeper, complained to the Halifax grand jury that the increase in the number of debtors being sentenced to jail had nibbled away at his yearly income. He sought regular compensation: in other words, a salary. The grand jury agreed to pay him fifty pounds a year, providing he collected no prisoner fees.

Ten years later, despite the fifty-pound salary, John Fielding, the new keeper of the Halifax "Bridewell," was still losing money. In December 1828, he told the Nova Scotia government that too many paupers were being sentenced to jail, many of them for paltry debts. If they could not pay off a small debt on the outside, they certainly could not afford to buy food and clothing once imprisoned. Fielding petitioned for an increase in his salary because he was feeding the starving wretches at his own expense.

Most keepers were not as kindly as John Fielding, and some were as downright raw and miserable as the living conditions in the jail.

Robert and David Angus cruelly beat prisoners just for the pleasure of it. They also stole food from the inmates who relied on charitable handouts to stay alive. A grand jury investigating these two jail keepers reported that the Angus brothers left "...a number of helpless prisoners almost to a state of starvation."

Not much improved over the years. In 1835, another grand jury reported that prisoners "...suffer from want of clothing. At night, they have a few ragged blankets barely one for each prisoner, and these swarming with vermin to a degree beyond belief."

New Brunswick had its share of "black holes." In 1821, a thirty-two-year-old man, Israel Perley of Salem, Massachusetts, was found guilty of debt and thrown into the St. Andrews jail for fifteen months. On August 4, 1822, he died. A coroner's inquest followed, and the St. Andrews newspaper, the *Herald*, reported its findings: "That Israel Perley died of the visitation of God. His death was hastened...by his confinement to the lower room of the jail...where he was exposed for three months to a pestilential effluvia arising from the privy in said room which occasioned insanity and disease by which he came to his death."

In 1875, Saint John had five lock-ups. A newspaperman visiting these reported that most were merely filthy dungeons, unfit for the lowliest beast. Most cells measured about eight by eight feet, and six feet in height. They were without light, and the only ventilation came from a hole in the ceiling and the cracks between the floorboards.

These were not heated, and were cleaned once a year—except for the lock-up on Duke Street, which had a floor so rotted it could not be scrubbed. The place, the reporter said, stank so foully that police staffing it had to eat their lunches out in the street.

And lest we forget, as late as 1909, the Saint John jail was still putting men to work in chain gangs.

Today's prisons are over-crowded, mind-numbing, deplorable institutions, but for sheer human misery, they don't hold a candle to prisons in the past.

FOGBOUND AND UNCIVILIZED

Joshua Marsden was a Methodist missionary who travelled the Maritimes preaching the word of God from 1801 to 1809. He liked some towns and settlements well enough, and some he could not abide. One he did not care for was Digby, Nova Scotia.

About Digby, Marsden writes:

> Arrived at Digby in the Bay of Fundy. As it was the Sabbath, I went ashore hoping for some opening to preach the Gospel. But, alas, Jesus Christ did not appear to have one foot of ground in all of Digby. After a solitary walk, I returned onboard the boat.
>
> Digby is given up to smuggling. At night, when the smugglers came on board to carry their contraband goods ashore, I was greatly disturbed with their profane and worldly conversation. At last I reproved them, but this brought upon me a flood of reproach and invective. I believe had it not been for fear of the consequences, they would have murdered me then and there.

The next day, Marsden boarded another boat for Annapolis Royal, which was a quiet, God-fearing town compared to Digby. Shortly after, he sailed for Saint John, New Brunswick. He writes:

"On my arrival at Saint John, the severity of the fog (sometimes the sun did not appear for a whole week) created great pulmonary oppression and difficulty of breathing. The climate appeared hostile to my constitution and occasioned a fear that eventually I should not be able to stand it."

That was written nearly two hundred years ago. In that time, Digby has become civilized, law-abiding, and God-fearing. As for Saint John, that nasty fog is still there.

PHILIP MARCHINGTON

Philip Marchington landed in Halifax in 1783 with a fortune in gold coins. He had made his money at what he called "general business"—selling supplies, slaves, and women to the British Army during the American Revolution.

Almost immediately, Marchington bought an entire block of property near the waterfront between Bell's Lane and Jacob Street, where he conducted more "general business." Marchington profited from his Loyalist connections. But those connections could not protect him from being expelled from the Methodist community for "attempting to raise himself above all discipline." The businessman retaliated by opening his own Methodist church on the property, and appointed himself preacher. He preached rousing sermons that attracted a sizable congregation.

In 1789, Marchington's wife suddenly died. He had been devoted to his wife. He doted on her throughout their married life, calling her "Dear Jane" in private and in public. It seems Marchington could not bear the loss of "Dear Jane," so he had her body encased in a glass coffin that he stored beside the pulpit in his church. Marchington gazed upon his dead wife daily.

Months passed. At last the grisly sight of the body decaying under glass and the overwhelming stench became too much for the congregation. Marchington's flock forced him to give "Dear Jane" a proper Christian burial.

Marchington began drinking heavily after that, as well as chasing the female members of his congregation. Haligonians started calling his church "Sodom."

His congregation dwindled, and soon he found himself preaching before empty pews. So he padlocked the door and returned to doing what he had always done best—making money in "general business."

ELIZABETH BEARD

A New Brunswick regiment of the line, the 104th, force-marched through driving snow from Fredericton, New Brunswick, up the St. John River, across Madawaska County, and down through Quebec. It was one "Christer" of a march. Hard slogging every step: fifty-two days, seven hundred miles, through blown and drifted snow and into a freezing northwest wind that could snuff the fires of hell. They reached Kingston, Ontario, on April 12, 1813, just in time to help stand off and push back an American invasion of Canada. This was during the War of 1812, a war to settle some of the old squabbles between the Americans and the British left over from the American Revolution.

The 104th took heavy casualties at Stoney Creek, Lundy's Lane, and the siege of Fort Erie. In those battles, the regiment did itself proud and earned a reputation for grit and hard fighting. Many of its rankers were New Brunswick boys, and six of them were the sons of the same woman—Elizabeth Beard Jasper Woodward Hopkins. Though their fathers had been soldiers themselves, the six sons came by their bravery and their tough-bitten willingness to fight from their mother. She had suffered more war and fought more battles than her three husbands and six soldier sons combined.

Elizabeth Beard was born in Philadelphia in 1761 and grew up watching street brawls and riots. During the 1760s and 70s, Philadelphia shared with Boston the limelight for political protest. Like Boston, Philadelphia also had a population churning for freedom and independence. These were the Patriots, the Sons of Liberty who rioted against British rule and against those Tories who supported it. Most were true believers in this cause of independence. Some, however, were street toughs and hooligans who served as muscle for radical politicians. These were the ones who silenced the conflict of words with shouts and drumbeats, and expressed their strong opinions with cudgels and clubs.

Elizabeth grew to womanhood in a Philadelphia household loyal to the Crown. There she heard about the tar and featherings of Loyalist friends and neighbours. Quickly, Elizabeth learned to despise these angry Americans. She openly sneered at them. In 1773, she showed her contempt for their loud-mouthed gripes against everything British by marrying John Jasper, a sergeant in His Majesty's army.

In 1776, the American Revolution turned the whole world upside down, including the world of young Elizabeth Beard Jasper. Almost overnight, she went from mistress of a garrison cabin in Philadelphia to one of thousands of camp followers pulling steady at dray carts loaded with baggage and living in the tramped mud of a bivouac. By then, she had two children already hanging on her skirts. With them in tow, she trailed her husband and his regiment through the blast and blue smoke of that war for independence.

She saw fighting up close: the flash of scarlet and blue coats against a green meadow, the entrenchments and assaults, and the neat rows and ranks breaking under grapeshot and volley. She witnessed the shout and lather of battle with its close-order gleam of bayonets. And she smelled the running blood and saw the smoke-blackened faces of boys not much older than herself. And at night, when the muskets and howitzers fell silent, she saw the torn tunics and scuffed boots of the soldiers, slow on their return, uncertain and wavering among the conical-shaped caps blowing over the battleground. In the firelight, she saw the wounds of the wounded and the twisted stares of the dead. And her marrow thickened and her spirit hardened at the sight of it all.

By 1779, the war had spread throughout all of His Majesty's North American colonies, from the Green Mountains of Vermont to the Florida swamps, from the marshlands of Nova Scotia to the steamy island of Jamaica, where a garrison of redcoats was under attack and desperate for reinforcement.

John Jasper was among the regiment of reinforcements who were seasick on board the brig *Stanley*, which had sailed a sea chop from New York Harbor and around Cape Hatteras. His family sailed with him. There was risk in Elizabeth sailing with her husband, of course, but not much more than the risk the war brought to the doorsteps of most Loyalists. Besides, there was something exciting in braving the danger of a few days' sail to the Caribbean under the supreme protection of His Majesty's navy. Or so she thought until that summer morning in 1779 when three French frigates (recent allies of the American rebels) sailed from the sunrise with cannons blistering the sea broadside the British ship.

The *Stanley* returned the cannonade, smashing chain shot into the mast and rigging of one ship and a cannonball through the upper deck of another. The third French attacker, however, closed and crossed the beam of the *Stanley*. It raked the *Stanley* with deck cannon and sniped at the *Stanley*'s crew with a volley from musketeers leg-locked in the main stays. Two dozen British sailors and soldiers went down with the volley, leaving several cannon unmanned.

That's when Elizabeth took a hand in the fighting. She helped man (or woman) one of those big guns. She charged the cannon with canister, loaded it with shot and ball, and plugged her ears at the blast. Then she lifted another twelve-pound cannonball into the muzzle. The brass barrel weighed a hundred pounds, and the truck a hundred more. These she and a sailor rope-hauled to the gunwale for another blast. Then another. And another, until the mind blotted out all but the back-bending effort of loading and firing, until the sky and the sea became one in what seemed a jelly bag of black smoke.

By midday, the *Stanley* had fought off the French attackers and limped for Jamaica with a deck load of wounded. Elizabeth was one of them.

Here, Elizabeth's memory confuses the details of what happened next. It seems that after nine months in Jamaica, with Elizabeth recovered from her wound, the family sailed for New York. They never made it. Their ship foundered off the New Jersey coast and put in at Cape May. There, American militia lay in ambush and captured John Jasper and his family, imprisoning them with twenty-two Loyalists at Morristown.

Somehow, Elizabeth escaped the jail. Or was set free, perhaps because of the children, or perhaps because a guard took kindly to her womanly charm. However it was, a few days later, Elizabeth returned to the Morristown jail with as many guns as she could carry. She slipped them to the prisoners one night, and the following day they fought their way to freedom.

In the gun battle and flight that followed, Elizabeth took a sword wound in her left arm from rebel cavalry. Still she ran, with one child in her arms and the other at her skirts, through the prickle and scratch of thick underbrush and across the open danger of flat-backed fields. A company of rebel soldiers saw her and one of them gave chase. A scuffle ensued. Elizabeth grabbed her pursuer's gun and shot him dead.

All of us live two lives—the life lived, and the life remembered. One wonders how Elizabeth truly remembered the close-up killing of that American soldier. Was it as cold and matter-of-fact as her deposition to the Commission for Loyalist Losses and Services suggests? Had the long years of war hardened her against sorrow? Or were those words in the deposition strictly the notations of a commissioner who had gleaned the facts from her story and recorded them? Had the commissioner left most of this woman's sentiment between the lines? Had the commissioner noticed but not recorded the tremor in her voice as she remembered the killing? Remembered the trouble in her pace on the march to New York, the uncertainty in her step, her pallid stare, her voice unwilling to speak for days?

Those days, and the six months that followed, seemed short from the hurry to get everything packed and everyone ready for their next journey. By December 1780, Sergeant Jasper and family were again on a voyage to Jamaica, then on to Pensacola in western Florida. At this British outpost in Pensacola, Jasper took malaria and died. He left his wife and family with little else but the clothes on their backs. He also left them squeezed among the army and refugee Loyalists within the palisade of Fort George, nervously awaiting a siege that was certain to come.

And come it did, in March 1781. General Bernardo de Gálvez, commander of a combined force of Spaniards, French, and American Patriots from Georgia and Louisiana, sailed into Pensacola Bay, disembarked nine thousand soldiers—along with mortars, cannon, and howitzers—and laid Pensacola under siege.

Among the twenty-five hundred defenders of Fort George was a small contingent of Maryland Loyalists. Elizabeth served with them. She took her turn at the twenty-four-pound cannon and fought alongside a Baltimore man named Samuel Woodward. For days on end, they shared the mud and smoke, the musket snipe, and the pounding from enemy artillery. Together they fixed powder and ball, rammed home wadding to compress the powder, threaded quick match (a strip of flannel soaked in wine) to the charge, and touched it with hellfire that blasted the cylinder and rolled like thunder.

For two months, they fought side by side, cheering and sorrowing in breaths. For two months, they lived together in the trenches of Fort George, together easing the terror of Elizabeth's children and scrounging and sharing what little there was to eat. For two months, they withstood the siege together, bruised and bloody, suffering with the wounded and burying the dead.

But two months was more siege than Elizabeth and Sam and most Pensacola defenders were willing to take. So on May 8, 1781, after a hot shell rolled into the powder magazine at the Queen's Redoubt and blew mangled bodies to hell and back, the Pensacola defenders more than willingly gave in and surrendered.

Two days later, Elizabeth and Sam got married. Their honeymoon was a hay barn on the outskirts of Pensacola and two years of Florida exile with thousands of other refugee Loyalists.

On October 17, 1781, the war for American independence ended, officially lost by General Cornwallis at Yorktown. It was another month before word spread to every corner of the colonies, and to the refugee Loyalists living in Florida. These Loyalists anxiously awaited the signing of the peace and the fulfillment of His Majesty's promise to resettle them in a colony un-pestered by war.

In late September 1783, Elizabeth Beard Jasper Woodward, with husband Sam and family, boarded the transport ship *Martha* and weighed anchor for Saint John, New Brunswick. The *Martha* carried more than three hundred on board, mostly Maryland Loyalists, but also some New Yorkers of DeLancey's Brigade. It safely followed the coast around Cape Cod, past the Dry Salvages (the ragged rocks off Cape Ann), and into the Gulf of Maine.

By day and by night, the sea spoke to the passengers in howls and yelps, in the whine in the rigging, in the cry of the gulls, and in the menace of the surf breaking on a shore still distant, but seeming closer and closer in the darkness. Despite the cool air, Elizabeth, Sam, and her youngest child lay on deck, listening to the voices of the sea. Perhaps winding up the past in their minds and trying to unravel the future. Perhaps measuring God's time in the back-and-forth roll of the ship.

There were others on deck that night, and they too woke to the pounding of breakers on the rocks that jutted from the water like granite teeth. On a tail of wind, they saw the froth and spume and sea-swelling centre churning on the reefs of the Seal Islands. They shouted a warning, but their voices were drowned in the crash and splinter of wood, and in the rush of water over the gunwales and filling the deck below.

Captain Patrick Kennedy of the Maryland Loyalists later swore at an official inquiry that the ship's captain had no business sailing at night. Not when they had sighted land before sunset. Not when they had heard the surf on the Seal Islands. Kennedy also swore that the captain and crew abandoned ship and pulled for shore in the jolly boat while passengers crowded the deck and cried for rescue.

Of the three hundred on board, only thirty-two men, two women, and one child were saved. While the rest tried and failed to make shore, Elizabeth, Sam, and her youngest son hung onto the wreck. After three days of this, fishermen from Marblehead, Massachusetts, landed them on the New Brunswick coast.

Some said what God had taken from Elizabeth with one hand, He had returned to her with the other. She had lost three children in the wreck of the *Martha*, but a few days after her rescue, she gave birth to triplets.

Triplets! Three boys! A three-in-one birth that did not give Elizabeth much time to grieve. Neither did the coming winter. Most Loyalists had arrived in New Brunswick over the past spring and summer, in time to plant a crop for winter and chop trees for a snug log cabin. The Woodwards, however, were among the late-coming Loyalists. By the time they canoed up the St. John River to their land grant in Block One, across the river from St. Ann's Point (Fredericton), it was late autumn. The brilliant orange and bright yellow leaves had already dulled and dried and fallen to a crunch on the forest floor. Winter was upon them before they knew it. And all they had to keep out the cold was a board hut banked with spruce boughs and a dug pit in the centre for a fire.

With three newborns in her arms, each squalling for a breast of milk, and a young son shivering at her skirts and bleating himself for something more to eat, Elizabeth must have wondered if suffering had permanently fixed itself in her life, and whether a single moment of God-blessed comfort would ever come her way.

It did. Comfort came with the spring freshet and the hot New Brunswick summer. It grew like the fiddlehead fern along the riverbank, and like the wheat and corn sprouting from the rich earth along the St. John River Valley.

So Elizabeth and family settled into the life of the St. John River. It was a quiet life, and a comfortable one.

When number-two husband Samuel died a bit later, Elizabeth married yet again—this time to Sergeant Jeremiah Hopkins, who later served in the 104th by the sides of two of his own sons, and four of his wife's. He remained in Fredericton when their boys marched off to fight in southern Ontario. And he was at her side in 1814 when the boys marched home.

The boys had soldier stories to tell about the hard march, and the hard drinking, and the hard-headed women they had met along the way. And as the night wore on, the fire died, and the dog irons cooled, they told about the hard fighting against the Yankees and how the fixed stares of the dead had jellied their bones.

Elizabeth knew to separate soldier talk from what was spoken from the heart. She recognized when bragging was a disguise for hurt. That's because she understood well enough what her boys had seen and experienced on a battlefield. If Elizabeth Beard Jasper Woodward Hopkins knew anything, she knew all about war, and death, and heartache. She had fought in three military engagements, married three soldiers, borne them four daughters and eighteen sons, lost several of her children to sickness and the sea, and cheated death herself more times than most care to think about. She knew that a life full of dare and danger had a downside of sorrow. And she knew when a war was over, it was best to shove aside the hurt and get on with the business of living.

She knew this because that's what she had done herself. Like so many soldiers who bore ragged scars from a country at war, she had folded and tucked her past into a neat bundle of memory, and lived out the rest of her days simply and happily on the St. John River.

BILL MCLEAN: A GOOD EXAMPLE

Thousands of Loyalists fled to the Maritimes after the British defeat in the American Revolution. By 1782, Halifax's population had doubled. Jobs and food were scarce. Poverty and hunger drove men and women to theft, robbery, prostitution, and all sorts of petty crimes and misdemeanours. The Halifax streets were unsafe day and night. The general public cried out for the courts and government to do something. It did. The government hanged Bill McLean.

Bill McLean was a Loyalist, a poor man with a wife and family to feed. When an opportunity presented itself, he took it—six pence from the change bowl of a fishmonger. Six pence! That was hardly enough for a week's worth of bread and molasses. Yet the Nova Scotia Supreme Court sentenced him to hang by the neck until dead.

After the sentencing, the grand jury had second thoughts about the charge and verdict. The jury petitioned the governor and Executive Council (the governing body of the day) for mercy, explaining that the criminal charge against McLean should have been for petty larceny and not for street robbery.

The difference in criminal charge meant a big difference in punishment. Petty larceny brought a punishment of thirty-nine lashes at the public whipping post, while street robbery resulted in a sentence of execution. But the Executive Council had no sympathy for the grand jury's petition. It ruled: "at present time when robberies have become so frequent, it is unavoidably necessary that William McLean should suffer for the sake of an example."

On November 5, 1782, Bill McLean kicked through the fallen leaves to the execution ground behind Citadel Hill. The morning sky was a blade of cold steel. The air stank of boiled sausage from the breakfast pots of the army bivouac at Camp Hill. Whether he deserved it or not, on that day Bill McLean was hanged for the sake of example.

UNUSUAL BAPTISM

(BJG)

In 1868, an evangelist named Mr. Coleman, a remarkable soul-saver, travelled through Queen's County, New Brunswick. He achieved great success at Cambridge Narrows, a community at the only fairly narrow spot in Washademoak Lake. It is at Cambridge Narrows that the current in the Washademoak sweeps around opposing points of land with surprising force.

On the morning appointed for the baptism, volunteers with axes chopped a channel about twelve feet out into the frozen lake, then enlarged its outer end into what was called the "Holy Hole." This hole in the ice was where the dipping of the recently saved took place.

After the usual sermon and exhortation—a powerful one urging the unsaved into redemption—the Reverend Mr. Coleman led his congregation, and those about to put on the mantle of salvation, down to the Holy Hole.

The first candidate was an elderly woman. Mr. Coleman led her into the water. It was bitterly cold; but the warmth of the spirit seemed to cancel it out. He pronounced the blessing, then dipped the woman. But in doing so, he slipped and lost his footing and his grip on the old woman. The strong current swept the poor soul away under the ice, and she was lost from the world forever.

The crowd on the bank gasped in horror, but Mr. Coleman turned to them in perfect composure. He raised his eyes to heaven, then said: "The Lord giveth and the Lord taketh away. Hand me another one."

ABANDONED BOYS

Irish immigrants, like so many immigrants, paid all they had for passage to Canadian ports. They set their minds and hearts and all their finances to sail to Canada's principal ports of Halifax, Saint John, and Montreal in search of a new life, a good life where food was plentiful and work ready to be had. Or so the immigrants wanted to believe.

In September 1817, Irish immigrants huddled on the waterfront in Dublin to wait their turn to board the *Harriett Hanna,* a cramped-looking ship that creaked sorrowfully with the tide. A man and wife with ten children stepped forward and laid a purse of hard coin on the captain's table. The captain counted it and determined there was hardly enough to pay passage for eight children—not ten. The mother's voice cracked as she begged the captain to take the family for what money they had. The captain thought a moment, bargained for the family to pay with future wages, then waved the family aboard.

The *Harriett Hanna* sailed out of Dublin with her decks filled to capacity. The ship had sailed the Irish coast for about one hundred miles when it stopped for provisions before breaking for the open sea.

Two men stood on the dock, each with enough hard coin for passage to the colonies. The captain, greedy for money in hand, welcomed the two men on board. Then he collared the two boys to whom he had granted passage for future payment, and put them ashore without telling their mother.

It was said the mother followed the ship's wake day and night. And when the *Harriett Hanna* anchored in Charlottetown, Prince Edward Island, for water and provisions before proceeding to Halifax, she ran ashore, her mind set on remaining there until she had earned enough money to return for her abandoned boys.

POVERTY

A description of the poor on Grand Manan and Campobello Island in the 1830s reads like a newspaper account of what today would be a third-world country. A reporter for the *St. Andrews Herald* described the almost inhuman state of people living on these islands.

Near the harbour, he said, there were four or five fishermen's huts without even chimneys. They did not have glass in the windows. The men, he said, fished only as much as they needed for enough rum "to deprive them of their senses." They had hardly enough food to make a meal for one, let alone for a family. As for their children, he reported that the younger ones ran about nude, and girls thirteen to sixteen years of age had only loincloths to cover themselves. "When a stranger appeared, all the youngsters scampered off and hid in the nearby woods; or, if surprised on the beach, lay down and tried to cover themselves with sand."

In 1811, Joshua Marsden, an itinerant preacher, wrote: "I have often been surprised at the inhabitants of Nova Scotia and New Brunswick, many of whom, though possessing considerable land, will live in these wretched hovels, sometimes with scarcely a pane of glass in the window, and frequently in the midst of winter the door wide open. One might almost imagine that such ice-hardened constitutions would be sufficiently inured to colonize the planet Saturn."

A traveller through Nova Scotia's backcountry in the 1820s describes a similar scene. Family after family of Irish immigrants lived in windowless, floorless hovels that they threw together to beat the December snow. A typical family's furnishings consisted of a broken bench, three broken crocks, some straw, and one old blanket shared by four.

Many of the poor were immigrants from abroad or fellow Maritimers travelling to Saint John and Halifax seeking work. On March 15, 1818, in a letter addressed to "Dear Sir," Peleg Wiswall, a Nova Scotia jurist, wrote: "Hordes of Paupers and Lazzaroni only come here to distress us and freeze and starve themselves." With little work to be had in either Saint John or Halifax, the poor were soon plucked off the streets and confined in the poorhouse, where they often spent the winter sharing a bunk and blanket with criminals and the insane.

On December 9, 1812, the Halifax grand jury reported that maintaining the transient poor was costing the city more than the four hundred pounds allotted by the provincial House of Assembly. It requested that liquor taxes go toward supporting the poor rather than maintaining county roads.

Increased immigration swelled the ranks of the poor. One Haligonian writing to the *Acadian Recorder* in 1827 wanted to stop the practice of bringing the poorest Irish to Nova Scotia. The writer suggested that ship captains provide financial security so their passengers would not become charges of the town. Other contributors to local newspapers demanded their provincial governments take a strong stand against immigration. They flat out wanted to send them back, the way Governor John Parr had done in 1789. Parr had written to the Lords of Trade: "Twenty poor wretches, mostly old and unable to earn a livelihood, recently arrived from Scotland, Ireland, and England. Since Halifax cannot support any more transient poor, the townsfolk contributed to send them back aboard the Brig Ark so their home parishes can take care of them."

Still Great Britain's poor continued to brave an ocean crossing, believing the streets in North America were paved with gold—only to find the alleys and avenues little more than byways of mud.

In 1832, the Halifax grand jury reported that the Asylum for the Poor "is too small to house the numbers now assembled there, nor is it fit for the various purposes it now serves." The building housed the poor, lunatics, and orphans. It also served as a hospital.

"In order to lose no space," the report continued, "children are put into beds with adults..."

The increasing numbers of poor and misbegotten had both Saint John and Halifax wrestling with the issue of caring for those unfortunates who came from elsewhere. In their local newspapers, many argued for their provincial governments to deny entry to impoverished immigrants, to load them back on the boats or show them the road out of town, telling them in no uncertain terms to return whence they came, to the wretched, starving lives they had left.

Peleg Wiswall wrote: "...the importation of many poor settlers will have a lasting effect in filling poor houses, raising the price of provisions, increasing crimes, bringing down the character of the Province, and eventually, furnishing recruits to the American Army and Navy."

STRONG STUFF

Isabel Robins was fourteen, and her brother John was ten, when their father, Richard Robins, left their home in New Jersey to settle a Loyalist land grant in Bedeque, Prince Edward Island. Their mother was dead, so the children stayed with an aunt, and anxiously waited to join their father.

Richard Robins often wrote to Isabel and John. He described the Island as the most beautiful place in the world. He said he was lonely, and that just as soon as his cabin was built and his farm returned a cash crop, he would send for them and the family would be reunited.

It took Richard Robins two years to settle his affairs and raise the money to pay for Isabel and John's passage. In 1784, they left New York and set sail for PEI by way of New Brunswick.

Isabel and John were a week sailing, then two weeks anchored in Passamaquoddy Bay waiting on weather, then another week making their way to Prince Edward Island. But as soon as their ship entered Bedeque Bay, the children recognized the place at once from the fine description in their father's letters.

A small boat rowed out to meet the ship, and John was certain one of the men in the boat was his father. He stood on the gunwale and waved until his arm ached. And when the boat drew near, young John called his father's name—Richard Robins.

The two men in the boat looked at each other strangely, and then the man at the oars called back: "We knew him. But he's dead. Two weeks ago this Sunday."

Like so many Loyalists who settled these Maritime provinces, tragedy and hard times were much a part of John and Isabel's lives. And also like so many Loyalists, John and Isabel Robins were made of strong stuff. They settled their father's land and made it prosper.

HENRY MOSS'S TAVERN

It is not unusual these days for Maritime taverns and bars to employ bands and singers to attract customers. Some stage singalongs of one sort or another, and others have male and female exotic dancers, scantily clad in little more than the altogether.

But during another era, in the 1860s, tastes were different and morals much more strict. No loud music or undressed dancers then. However, there was exotic spectacle for attracting the drinking clientele.

Henry Moss owned a saloon on Barrington Street in Halifax, Nova Scotia. He had plenty of competition. Halifax had more than its share of watering holes, and still does.

By 1869, Moss's stiff competition became fierce. Moss started losing business and decided he needed to do something fast. That's when he hit on the idea of entertainment—something exotic, a spectacle that would excite the imagination and lure customers away from his competitors.

This ad appeared in the Halifax newspaper: "On exhibit at Moss's Tavern, Saloon, and Dining Hall! The accoutrements worn by the warriors of some Asiatic and African savage tribes."

Henry Moss even had a wax figure sculpted and dressed in these curiosities. Halifax drinkers crowded into Moss's Tavern for a close-up look at this spectacle, and Henry Moss was back in business.

Within a month, other tavern owners had their own exotic entertainment. One staged a magnesium light display, another played a phonograph, and another offered a small library of old and rare books. Now, this tavern owner with the library, he must have been a real wild man.

EARLY TOURISTS

Today Prince Edward Island is a tourist mecca, but that was not always so.

In the eighteenth century, the most valuable lands on PEI were held by absentee landlords who sent hired favourites to run their overseas estates, while they sat in London and collected rents.

Almost the only people who stayed on the Island were the military, and those who had nowhere else to go.

Loyalist Benjamin Marston of Marblehead, Massachusetts, visited on June 11, 1786. He recorded this in his diary:

"...arrived at Charlottetown. A very poor, miserable place, as all must be which are inhabited by the idle, indolent, poor gentry—who are at perpetual variance among themselves and ready to take advantage of all who come among them."

Thirty-six years later, in 1822, William Johnstone offered this picture of Charlottetown: "...tidily laid out in main streets 80 feet wide and cross-streets 40 feet. There is a large square in the middle of the town, where the Courthouse, the High Church, and Market House stand, with plenty of open ground for drilling militia and holding executions."

In 1855, an Englishwoman, Isabella Bird, visited the Island, and here's part of her description: "It may be remarked, however, that society is not on so safe a footing as in England. Such things as duels, but of a very bloodless nature, have been known; people occasionally horsewhip and kick each other; and if a gentleman indulges in the pastime of breaking the windows of another gentleman, he receives a bullet for his pains."

Today, it is something of a comfort to Islanders that they can boast of some measure of progress in these 160-odd years.

REVENGE

In Saint John, New Brunswick, in the spring of 1789, James Christian, captain of the sloop *Betsy*, acquired a black man named John Robinson at a bargain price. Robinson stood before a Saint John court on a charge of stealing two screws from a carpentry shop where he worked. Instead of sentencing Robinson to jail, the judge determined Robinson was more a public nuisance than a criminal, and ordered him bound out as an indentured servant, which was one step short of being a slave.

Captain James Christian recognized a bargain when he saw one. He accepted Robinson's bond in exchange for providing Robinson with food, clothing, and accommodation.

Captain Christian was a hard master. His orders often came on the toe end of his boot, his encouragement with the sharp bite of a leather whip.

The *Betsy* sailed the coastline to the West Indies for a load of sugar cane and molasses at St. Kitts. Then, at Old Road, under Captain Christian's watchful eye, Robinson loaded case after case of rum and raw-headed gin on board and stored it in the afterpart of the vessel, under the cabin in a place called the "run." Then the *Betsy* weighed anchor for Halifax.

During the return voyage, the captain, wild and cruel from drink, snapped his whip on Robinson's back again and again, hardening Robinson's resolve to seek revenge.

On June 29, 1789, the *Betsy* dropped anchor in Halifax, and a tidewaiter (a customs officer) boarded the vessel. Captain Christian declared a cargo of molasses and sugar cane, but about the rum and gin he said not a word.

That night, Robinson rowed Captain Christian in a dinghy loaded with the rum and gin to Mr. Freeman's store near the Market Wharf at the foot of George Street. No sooner had Robinson stored the booze in Freeman's cellar than the bond servant, feeling the painful scars on his back and remembering the countless beatings while at sea, dropped his oar on the beach and ran for a magistrate.

John Robinson testified in vice-admiralty court against Captain James Christian. He told the judge about the voyage to St. Kitts, the loading of rum and gin at Old Road, and about selling the smuggled booze to Mr. Freeman. The judge convicted Christian of smuggling, fined him fifty pounds, and sentenced him to fifty lashes at the public whipping post.

John Robinson stood at the Market Wharf and watched the sheriff tie Captain James Christian to the red-painted post, and damn near smiled as the cat-o'-nine-tails cut a criss-cross pattern into the back of his former master.

"Serves him right," several overheard John Robinson say. And by that, they knew what Robinson meant—that Captain James Christian was getting all that he had bargained for.

A LATE-SUMMER RIOT

Barrack Street (now Brunswick Street) in Halifax was rowdy at the best of times. It ran between the North and South Barracks in the upper part of town near the Citadel, and was a stretch of whorehouses and taverns. At night, it was generally packed shoulder-to-shoulder with soldiers and sailors engaged in drinking, whoring, dancing, and fighting.

One night, August 31, 1838, a sailor off HMS *Dolphin* had one of Richard Coopers's whores refuse him service for which he had already paid. He complained to the owner and received a beating in return. The owner then bounced the sailor into a back alley and ordered him on his way.

Early the following night, a group of fellow sailors sought revenge for their mate's "ill-use," but Police Magistrate John Liddell and three constables, responding to a rumour of more trouble than usual on Barrack Street, intercepted the sailors and ordered them back to their ship. The sailors, however, were resolved to get even, and at ten o'clock returned to Barrack Street, entered Cooper's Tavern, and accused the owner of robbing their mate the night before. Several soldiers intervened, and all of a sudden, all hell broke loose. The soldiers gleefully tossed the sailors out a second-floor window, followed by their clothing, then the beds and chairs from the various rooms.

Their wildness was infectious. Other soldiers who had watched the free-for-all from the street now stormed into Cooper's joint to share in the fun. They ripped and pried free floorboards and wallboards and tossed them out, followed by floor joists and rafters. The roof collapsed and the walls fell out. More than twenty soldiers and a dozen half-naked women tumbled into the street.

With their hearts pumping for more destruction, the soldiers charged down Barrack Street to Cook's Tavern, and within twenty minutes tore it to the ground.

By now, townsfolk had gathered on Citadel Hill, and they cheered the soldiers on, calling out the names of taverns and whorehouses the soldiers should tear down next. Thornham's Bawdy House crashed to the ground, spilling soldiers, sailors, whores, and private citizens into the warm summer night.

The townsfolk cheered and cheered, and stayed up all night watching the wholesale destruction.

With daylight came peace and calm. But it was not until midday, when the soldiers roused from their bunks, that they realized what they had done. In one wild night, they had accomplished what the city government had failed to do for years—they had put out of business half a dozen of Halifax's most infamous places of sin.

SHORT STRAW

In the spring of 1813, a small fishing vessel, the *Young William,* sailed into Halifax Harbour, returning to port after rescuing several starved and raggedly dressed sailors from the abandoned ship *Serphina.*

The captain of the *Serphina* was missing, and Halifax authorities suspected mutiny and murder. A commission made up of Richard John Uniacke, the attorney general for Nova Scotia, and Michael Wallace, a member of the Executive Council, investigated the case. What they discovered was shocking.

The *Serphina* had sailed out of New York in early April, and within two days at sea had run into a bad storm that shredded canvas and shattered timber. The ship capsized, and the captain ordered the mast and rigging chopped away so the ship could right herself. Provisions had washed overboard, and now, with t+he mast and rigging gone, the ship drifted helplessly on the open sea.

After several days of desperate hunger, the captain ordered "a lottery" in which each crew member, including himself, would draw straws to determine who would be first to be killed and eaten.

The captain went first, and, to the amazement of all on board, he drew the short straw. Without hesitation, the captain removed his silver watch and entrusted it to James Harris, the *Serphina*'s only passenger. Then he undressed, folded his clothes, and offered himself for execution.

Over the next week, the survivors cannibalized five more men.

The Halifax commissioners, Uniacke and Wallace, listened to the evidence as stoically as humanly possible and then dismissed all charges of mutiny and murder. They based their decision on the testimony of James Harris, who swore the lottery and cannibalism had been initiated and conducted according to the captain's orders.

SLAVERY

Most associate slavery with the southern part of the United States, and few ever think that slavery was practiced in our own backyard. Sadly, it was.

On May 30, 1752, Joshua Mauger, a prominent businessman and member of the Nova Scotia Executive Council, advertised in the *Halifax Gazette* that he was selling a "negro wench and a creole boy" at Lockhart's Store. And on November 1, 1760, this advertisement appeared in the same newspaper: "To be sold at public auction, on Monday the 3rd of November, at the house of Mr. John Rider, two slaves, viz.: a boy and girl about eleven years old; likewise, a puncheon of choice old cherry brandy, with sundry other articles."

In 1774 when a black woman sued for her freedom in a Nova Scotia court, Chief Justice Blowers immediately dismissed the case without comment, an act that clearly supported the slave owner. In Shelburne, Nova Scotia, Jesse Gray sold a slave named Mary Postill for 150 bushels of potatoes.

In 1800, a black slave named Nancy came before a New Brunswick court seeking her freedom. But the court offered no decision, and returned Nancy to her owner, William Bailey. This case, however, so bothered the conscience of Judge Isaac Allen that at the trial's conclusion, he set free all of his own slaves.

A year after, in Nova Scotia, the last will and testament of Benjamin Belcher was upheld in court, and his family carried out his wishes.

"I give and bequeath my negro boy, Prince, to my son, Stephen Belcher, during his lifetime, after that to his eldest surviving son; my negro girl, Dianna, to my daughter, Elizabeth Belcher Sheffield, and after her death to her eldest male heir. I give my negro man, named Jack and my negro boy Samuel and negro boy James and a negro girl named Chloe to my son, Benjamin Belcher, and his heirs, forever, charging them my children, unto whom I have entrusted these negro people with never to sell, barter, and exchange them."

Slavery continued in the Maritime provinces for decades after. And it was not until 1834 that slavery was made illegal in Britain's North American colonies.

A YOUNG PRIVATEER

In the eighteenth and nineteenth centuries, when the British went to war, they enlisted the support of privately owned warships. These were called "privateers," and they were licensed to attack and capture enemy ships, usually American, French, or Spanish. On the British side of the ledger, these privateers were legitimate fighting ships. On the enemy side, the privateers were pirates, plain and simple.

Privateering was often a boy's romantic dream. It meant adventure, glory, and pockets bulging with gold coins.

In 1805, Thomas Barnaby from Liverpool, Nova Scotia, had high hopes for gold and glory when he boarded the *Charles and Mary Wentworth*, a local privateer bound for the Caribbean.

On June 5, they captured a Spanish schooner loaded with silver bars, tobacco, and rum—a valuable prize. The captain left Thomas Barnaby and several others to sail the prize ship back to Nova Scotia. On the first night of their return voyage, a storm separated the prize ship from the *Charles and Mary Wentworth*, and the next day a Spanish warship attacked and re-captured the prize schooner.

All of a sudden the glory was gone from a privateering life, and the adventure turned into a nightmare for Thomas Barnaby. He was now a prisoner, no longer the dashing Nova Scotia privateer, but, in Spanish eyes, a common pirate. And he was treated as one.

Without trial, the boy was locked in a dungeon in Colombia and left to rot away the last years of his life. He sent a letter to his family in Liverpool to tell them the fate of a captured privateer—it was prison, disease, and death. Then he wished them well and said "goodbye."

WOMEN'S INSURANCE BILL

(BJG)

The struggle for women's freedom has been long, and mostly uphill. Many women's rights that today we take for granted were hard in coming. It was like pulling teeth to get men to compromise for the benefit of women.

Take the political struggle over the women's insurance bill in New Brunswick in 1881. It demonstrates the stubborn unwillingness of many male legislators to budge one inch in granting women individual freedoms.

In 1881, Arthur Gilmore, MLA for Charlotte County, New Brunswick, introduced into the New Brunswick House of Assembly a bill that granted women the right to be beneficiaries to their husbands' insurance policies. The bill met strong opposition, led by William End from Albert County.

William End argued that such a bill would give women an interest in their husbands' deaths, and that would put men always on guard against their wives—day and night.

Arthur Gilmore went red-faced with anger. He rose in the New Brunswick House and bellowed: "If women were not so forbearing, the majority of husbands would have been poisoned long ago."

Those words brought William End to his feet once again. To thunderous applause from his supporters, and with eyes ablaze with warning, William End recounted four cases from the courts in which women administered arsenic to their husbands. His dire warnings won some votes, but not enough. The women's insurance bill passed by a slim margin of seventeen to fifteen.

JOB APPLICATIONS

(BJG)

In 1921, Newman Clark languished in jail in Andover, New Brunswick, awaiting his official hanging for the murder of Phoebe

Bell nearly a year earlier. Sheriff Tibbits of Victoria County said the death penalty was scarcely pronounced when he began getting applications for the gallows job.

One came from a man named Ellis, but another fellow named Holmes offered as well, and Holmes could provide references. Ellis's price was one hundred dollars; Holmes said seventy-five.

Then somebody started a rumour that Sheriff Tibbits was offering one thousand dollars to hang Newman Clark. This brought an offer from a man in the backcountry, one whom the sheriff knew well. Sheriff Tibbits told a newspaper: "I wouldn't send for that fellow…'cause I don't think he could hang a cat and do it right."

In 1925, a man named William J. Stokes gave a different twist to applications for hangman.

Harry D. Williams was sentenced to the rope for the brutal slaying of two little girls near Fosterville in New Brunswick's York County. Sheriff John B. Hawthorn was due to head out for Montreal the very next day to hire a proper hangman when he received a letter from William J. Stokes.

Stokes wrote: "Why should they give the hangman's job to some fellow from Montreal when a Maritime man needs the work?"

Who-Bodies

and

Some-Bodies

AMOR DE COSMOS

Jesse and Charlotte Smith of Windsor, Nova Scotia, gave birth to a son on August 20, 1825, and named him William Alexander Smith. Little did they know their son was destined to be famous—but under another name.

When he was fifteen, Bill Smith and his parents moved to Halifax, where young Bill attended Dalhousie University, joined the debating club, and got caught up in Joseph Howe's political reform movement. Bill was a broadminded boy who wanted everything all at once—political change, adventure, wealth, and fame.

He was thirty-one when he got the urge for gold. He caught a boat to New York, a train to St. Louis, Missouri, and a covered wagon to Salt Lake City, Utah. There, he joined the Church of Latter Day Saints—the Mormons. He stayed for two years under the church's strict rule before continuing on to the California gold fields.

By this time, Bill Smith had come to think a great deal of himself, and very little about his name. There was nothing special about it, nothing that set him apart from so many others with plain, ordinary names.

So on February 15, 1854, by special bill of the California legislature, Bill Smith changed his name to Amor de Cosmos (Lover of the Universe), because of what he cared for most—"Love of order, beauty, the universal."

Amor de Cosmos then followed the gold fever to the Cariboo gold district of British Columbia. And when the gold played out, in 1858 he founded the *British Colonist* newspaper. He advocated public education and responsible government through an elected assembly. He also favoured Confederation for the colonies in Upper and Lower Canada and the Maritimes, and was responsible, years later, for bringing British Columbia into union with the other Canadian provinces. He has been called British Columbia's Father of Confederation.

In the 1872 provincial election, British Columbia elected Amor de Cosmos premier. He kept true to his earlier following of Joseph Howe and brought social and political reform to British Columbia. Later, he became the province's first member of the House of Commons in Ottawa.

When you think of it, Amor de Cosmos accomplished a great deal for a man born in Windsor, Nova Scotia, with such an ordinary name—Bill Smith.

SAM LANGFORD

Newspapers called him the Boston Tar Baby, but he was Nova Scotia born and raised, and one of the greatest boxers the fight game has ever known.

Sam Langford, a black man, was built like a fire hydrant and twice as hard. He fought between 1902 and 1917. Langford could hit a ton. He needed only six inches of punching space to rock an opponent to the mat.

In 1908, Sam was in San Francisco to fight the local champ, Fireman Jim Flynn. On fight day, a west coast sportswriter, H. M. Walker, wrote in his column that Jim Flynn was wasting his time fighting the likes of Sam Langford. "Why Flynn will chew that black fighter to bits," the sportswriter predicted.

Joe Woodman, Sam's manager, read that column to Langford in the locker room and watched the black fighter's eyes narrow. That night, Langford danced Jim Flynn around the canvas until he had him standing right above the sports desk. Sam let loose a four-punch combination that lifted Flynn off his feet, over the ropes, and sprawling into H. M. Walker's lap.

Sam wiped sweat from his face and smiled.

Sam fought Harry Wills, Sam McVey, and Joe Jeanette. They were the best boxers in the world at the time, and the only prizefighters brave enough to stand toe-to-toe with Sam Langford.

Even Jack Johnson, the reining champ, feared to climb into the same ring with Sam. The two men had fought once back in 1906, before Jack Johnson was champ. It had been a gruelling match, a regular slugfest that ended in a draw. When it was over, Johnson said Sam Langford could beat him any night of the week.

From then on, the only fighter Jack Johnson ever avoided was Sam Langford from Weymouth, Nova Scotia, one of the greatest boxers to lace on a pair of gloves.

COTTAGE CRAFT

She had shown exceptional artistic talent as a young girl in St. Andrew's, New Brunswick, and her parents had scraped and saved to send her to art school in New York City. When she landed back in St. Andrews in 1912, after her mother's death, folks figured she was a talent wasted. But that was not to be. With ten bucks in her pocket and a heart full of ambition, Grace Helen Mowat started the Charlotte County Cottage Craft. She set out to use her talent as an artist and designer by putting the colours of autumn leaves and ocean sunsets into hooked rugs and weaving.

She hired farmwives, who worked from their homes. They knew the business of hooking and weaving, and when they matched their down-home skills with Grace Mowat's designs, the final products were breathtaking spectacles of colour and heartfelt craftsmanship.

Almost at once, the business took off. And soon the label of the Charlotte County Cottage Craft was recognized at country fairs and in big-city department stores throughout North America. It became one of the biggest and most successful cottage industries in New Brunswick history.

Grace Helen Mowat had fulfilled her dream. She had set out to brighten the homes and inspire the lives of everyday folk with the spectacular and peaceful colours of nature. She did just that and more. Her dedication to design and craftsmanship silenced those who had once said she was "a talent wasted." Instead, her early critics sang her praises, bragging up her St. Andrew's roots, and exclaiming that every cent her parents shelled out for New York art lessons was money well spent.

STRONGMEN

John MacNeil settled in Big Beach, Cape Breton, in the early 1800s. He came from Barra, Scotland. He was a big man, a really big man. He was so big that folks called him "Goliath." And he was as strong as he was big. Whenever anything needed moving in Big Beach, John MacNeil was the first man called to move it.

The funny thing was—his boys were even stronger. At nineteen, Donald MacNeil, the oldest, was said to be able to move an enormous boulder with ease. The boulder lay in a back field, and each year at haying time, Donald moved the boulder to one side for the haymakers, then back again to make way for another swath. And he didn't just roll it aside. He lifted it with ease, the way another nineteen-year-old would lift a young girl at a barn dance.

Still, Donald MacNeil was not the strongest of the MacNeil family. Neil MacNeil was. He was thirteen years old when he came across a two-year-old heifer stuck in a bog. In its effort to get out, the heifer had completely disabled its hind legs. It was so deep in the mud there was no hope of it getting out on its own.

Neil MacNeil made a rope of birch sapling and tied the heifer's front and hind legs. Then he waded into the bog, found a firm bottom, and set his feet for freeing the animal from the muck. Neil put his head and shoulders through the loop of birch rope, hoisted the heifer on his shoulders, and carried her back to the barn.

John MacNeil had four daughters as well as his two sons. But the strength of those MacNeil girls—well, that's another story.

FLYING

When Robert McGowan walked the streets of Sydney, Cape Breton, folks flapped their arms at him and quacked like a duck. That's because the only thing Bob McGowan could think or talk about was flying—an airplane, that is. He wanted to build and fly the first 100 percent Canadian-made airplane.

Bob McGowan had always liked to tinker. In 1905, he worked as apprentice for a watchmaker in Sydney. The watchmaker was something of an inventor himself, and had constructed a crude gas turbine engine that would work, if only he could figure out how to inject and ignite the gas.

One day when the watchmaker was away, McGowan used compressed air to spew gas into the cylinder and when he ignited it—"The thing took off," McGowan remembered, "and it actually produced power...before it melted and set the shop on fire!"

That ended his watchmaking career. He now directed his full attention to aviation. He experimented with glider planes, and one of his gliders made a three-and-a-half-mile flight from Point Edward to Sydney. But in was in June 1911 that McGowan made history.

He had spent four years scrounging machine parts and metal from the Sydney Steel Plant. His engine was handmade with 100 percent Canadian labour and 100 percent Canadian material. And when he took to the air on that cool June morning in 1911, Robert McGowan was flying the original—Canada's first—airplane.

McGowan was truly a man ahead of his time. In 1931, he bought five Fokker seaplanes from the Hudson's Bay Company and formed the Maritime-Newfoundland Airways Company. He carried the Royal Mail throughout Atlantic Canada.

Robert McGowan was a Cape Breton boy with a dream he never let go. He wanted to fly—and he did.

ALDEN THE TALKER

Most Maritime roads in the 1860s were glorified cow paths. The only ones fit to travel were the coach roads, and these were so bumpy that a one-way trip often left a traveller with loose molars. The coach road from Saint John to Moncton was one of these. It bounced its way through Nauwigewauk, Hampton, Sussex, Petitcodiac, and Moncton.

The driver's name was Johnny Alden, a round-faced, fun-loving chap. Alden was a talker. Get him going and he could talk a minister out of church. He also chewed tobacco and often punctuated his sentences with a squirt of tobacco juice.

On one trip, a Mr. Gyles rode on the dickey seat beside Alden. Mr. Gyles was a high-and-mighty, stuffed-shirt Englishman, unaccustomed to the easy ways of the Maritimes. He preferred speaking only to those of his own class.

Alden spoke to anyone and everyone. He kept up a constant patter—talking and spitting his way along the coach road as it travelled beside the Kennebecasis River. Mr. Gyles tried ignoring the driver. He took to pulling up his shirt collar to hide his face, hoping that would quiet Alden's incessant prattle.

Alden felt the Englishman's cold shoulder. He was hurt that his friendly conversation was unappreciated, and worse—being ignored. Alden had even aimed his tobacco juice so the spray did not stain Mr. Gyles's highly polished boots.

Near the stage stop at Sussex, Alden tried one last time to curry the Englishman's favour, but Gyles would have none of it and further buried his face behind his shirt collar.

Alden leaned close, peeked over the shirt collar, and said: "If you pull up that shirt of yours any higher, you'll catch cold in your arse."

Mr. Gyles climbed from the stage in Sussex and swore he'd walk to Moncton before riding another mile with Johnny Alden.

FLORENCE MACDONALD

A 1928 newspaper headline read: "Cape Breton girl chases the gold for the U.S. Olympic team."

The girl was Florence MacDonald from French Road, Cape Breton. She ran what was once considered the most gruelling Olympic track and field event for women, the "eight-eighty"—880 metres of all-out effort.

Florence started her sports career as a swimmer, but in 1920 her family moved to Boston, and coaches there encouraged her to concentrate on track and field. She was eighteen at the time. Once she got started at running, Florence broke most U.S. records for the fifty-yard dash.

Florence had speed and stamina. She was a coach's dream. In 1927, her coach encouraged her to try the murderous eight-eighty. Florence worked hard to conquer an event that demanded so much effort from an athlete, but conquer it she did, and immediately won a berth on the U.S. Olympic team in Amsterdam.

At the 1928 Olympics, Florence ran the eight-eighty against the best female runners in the world. And she took them right down to the wire. She shaved a half-second off the world record—and still finished sixth.

Had Florence had a second shot at running the eight-eighty in the 1932 Olympics, she surely would have brought home gold. But shortly after the 1928 Olympics, the women's eight-eighty was banned from international competition. Women's groups lobbied against the race. They thought it too gruelling a sports event for women and a deterrent to motherhood.

DESERTERS

In the eighteenth and early nineteenth centuries, military service was next in line to a prison sentence. The life was hard and often very cruel. Desertion was commonplace. And if a dollar could be made off helping soldiers and sailors desert their posts, there were those able and willing to do so.

In 1825, Lieutenant Malcolm Brown had the dubious assignment of hunting down military deserters and capturing civilians who made a buck helping them. That summer, a soldier deserted from the 81st Regiment in Halifax, and Lieutenant Brown was hot on his trail. Brown knew the escape routes from Halifax. Deserters either stowed away on trading ships, or hightailed it out on the Cobequid Road for Truro, and then on to New Brunswick.

In early August, Brown heard about a down-and-out farmer in Musquodoboit who had recently hired a new man. The farmer's name was William Roberts, and he had a gravel-patch farm that hardly grew enough to keep one man busy, let alone two.

Lieutenant Brown went looking at Roberts's farm. The farmer barred the door, and only opened it when Lieutenant Brown drew a horse pistol and threatened to shoot.

Brown found a man hiding in the cellar. A deserter—only not the one Brown was after. This man was from the 96th Regiment.

Nevertheless, Lieutenant Brown collared both the deserter and William Roberts, and hauled them off to Halifax for trial and a stiff jail sentence.

On the way to Halifax, along the Cobequid Road, Lieutenant Brown stopped for the night at a nearby inn. He shackled his prisoners to an overhead beam and was about to settle himself, when he looked out the window and saw a man sneaking from the back door, wearing a red tunic and carrying a bedroll under his arm.

Brown charged his horse pistol and followed, keeping his distance until he could take the soldier by surprise. They walked about a mile, and then the soldier stepped from the road and into a clearing where he planned to settle for the night. Brown waited an hour or so before entering the clearing and waking the soldier by nudging the barrel of his pistol against the man's cheek. The soldier belonged to the 81st Regiment—the deserter Brown had originally been looking for.

JAMES FRASER

James Fraser was born aboard the *Hector*, the ship that landed settlers in Pictou, Nova Scotia, in 1773. It seems his birth at sea was an omen that he would live a daring and exciting seafaring life.

At twenty years old, Fraser went to sea aboard an American ship that traded between Boston and Mediterranean ports. While at anchor on the African coast, his shipmates ran afoul of Algerian law, and crew and captain were clapped in irons and confined in a disease-ridden jail. A fever broke out, and one after the next, the crew began dying.

James Fraser clung to life and outlasted the others. He was then sold into slavery to an elderly Algerian woman, regained his health, and one night escaped by swimming to a British ship anchored in the Algerian harbour. He sailed with the British ship for only a short time, and then caught passage on an American vessel that sailed him to Virginia.

Not long after, Fraser engaged in a secret and illegal trade. This was in 1808, and Europe was at war with Napoleon Bonaparte. Fraser served as first mate on a ship that represented American merchants and traded with both sides in the war.

Trade was good; it was very good. With his share of three barrels of gold coins on board, Fraser planned to reach Boston and retire for life. Fraser's ship was off the coast of France and heading home when a French cruiser spotted it, and drew alongside and boarded. It didn't matter that the Americans were neutral in this war, and that Fraser's ship was a merchantman. The French captain recognized value when he saw it. He claimed the merchantman as prize goods and confiscated the gold coins.

The French captain locked the merchant sailors in the hold and divided his own crew to sail the two ships for France. Before reaching port, James Fraser escaped the hold, slipped over the side, and swam for shore. He eventually made his way to Stockholm, and then to England.

While in England, James Fraser sent a letter to Napoleon asking for his money back, claiming that France and America were not at war and the boarding of his ship and confiscation of the loot was an unlawful search and seizure. There was no reply.

Fraser made another bold move in England. He got married. Later, with wife and child, he returned to Pictou, Nova Scotia, after a twenty-year absence and a thrilling life at sea.

However, seafaring was still not out of his blood. A few years later, when Mr. Mortimer offered him the command of a merchant vessel, Fraser signed on without a moment's hesitation. This was during the War of 1812, and American warships sailed these Maritime coasts preying on British merchant ships. No sooner had Fraser fitted out Mortimer's merchantman and put to sea than it was captured by Commodore Rogers of the American navy. Rogers transferred the cargo to his own ship, set the captured vessel on fire, and transported Fraser and his crew to the jail in Salem, Massachusetts.

James Fraser seemed to have a way of getting himself in and out of jails. After a year of incarceration, he and most of his crew escaped the Salem jail. They bushwhacked their way north to British territory in New Brunswick, and then on home to Pictou.

When asked about the loss of Mortimer's ship, in which Fraser held a sizable share, Fraser remarked: "Oh, it's just the fortune of war."

JIM BERRY

James Berry lived at Six Mile Brook, near Pictou, Nova Scotia. His life spanned nearly a century: born 1819, died 1906. And for every day of those eighty-seven years, he had to be one of the busiest human beings to set foot in the Maritimes.

Today we'd probably call Jim Barry a workaholic for the way he filled every waking moment with work. He lived in an era when a working day was longer, the work was harder, and when folks had to entertain themselves.

First, Jim Berry kept a daily diary—six volumes for fifty years. He carefully recorded his day-to-day activity in the clearest handwriting, which revealed a man of patience and precision.

He owned a sawmill and a gristmill, and worked as sawyer and miller mostly every day of every week. He also served as his own secretary and bookkeeper. When the nights got long and he wanted for something to do, Jim Berry built a printing press and handcrafted more than a thousand letters of type in various sizes and styles.

He started binding his own books. He tanned the leather covers himself. His house was floor-to-ceiling bookcases, each chockablock with books. And Jim Berry could neither read nor write. He just respected the mystery of books and the knowledge they contained, and wanted to preserve them for succeeding generations.

Still he had a minute here and there to spare, so he taught himself to play the violin. Soon he had invitations to play in Truro and Halifax. When he died, he left behind the mill business, the printing press and hand-crafted type, his multi-volume diary, and a music book of more than two thousand songs—all of which Jim Berry composed himself.

BELTY MURPHY

By the time she was fifty years old, in 1882, Elizabeth "Belty" Murphy's mind had gone the way of moonlight. She was harmless, mind you, though something of a pest in her way of locking eyes with passersby on Queen Street in Fredericton, New Brunswick, and winking and smiling that fun-loving smile of hers. Most folks knew who Belty was, and so just smiled back, nodded politely, and continued on their way. Some even bought the apples she was selling. Of course, within a block or so they would toss them away, because the apples might be poisoned or hexed or blighted from the crust of dirt on Belty's hands and face—and most likely on the rest of her bony body, though it was hard to tell, since she covered herself neck to knees with a ragbag of fashion. She was draped in more colour than a milliner's shop, all of it swaddled ten ways at once and hitched at the waist by that big brass buckle belt that had earned her the name "Belty."

The belt had belonged to her husband, Patsy Murphy, who had been a bare-knuckles prizefighter in New Brunswick during the 1840s and 50s. Patsy Murphy was a sticker. He stuck a fist into anyone and anything that got in his way. By the 1850s, he had fought his way out of hardship and to the top of the New Brunswick fight game. His name was known throughout most of the lower St. John River Valley. He would arrive in towns and villages by coach or riverboat, wearing the championship belt and showing off his ironbound body and quick fists. People cheered and cheered, and later that day laid down two pennies to watch him reshape another man's face.

Belty followed him from town to town, fight to fight, up and down the river with a child on her skirts. Saint John, Fredericton, Woodstock, Grand Falls. Sometimes they travelled by coach to Moncton, or by wagon to the logging camps on the Miramichi or the Nashwaak River.

In 1860, Patsy was forty-two and still toeing the line for prize money, still loading power into each punch, still needing only six inches of distance to take another man down. He still held the title and the big brass buckle belt that went with it. By this time, however, his brain had numbed from too many shots to the head. His hands shook, his legs wobbled, and he drank day and night to chase away the fear and the bogies that had him ducking shadows and imaginary punches.

In Fredericton, Belty took a job cooking for Colonel Harding of the 22nd Regiment. She made up for the money Patsy drank. Colonel Harding was a crusty Englishman with mutton chop whiskers and a demeanour as stiff and arrogant as only an English army officer can have. Yet they took to one another right off; Harding's reserve and spit-and-polish ways were a counterpunch to Belty's larky way of singing her thoughts and showing her feelings like lace on a new dress. She even got away with clobbering the colonel with a right hook because Harding had asked her to fix him a bowl of bony clabber for dinner. Belty thought this was a lewd remark, and straightened up the colonel with a short punch thrown from her thighs the way Patsy had shown her.

Colonel Harding sat down dazed and apologetic for what he had said or for what Belty thought he had said. He even raised her pay one penny a week—though it did her little good, because a month later Patsy died and she stopped working.

It was early one autumn evening. Belty had kicked her way home through the dry leaves blowing in the street. She found Patsy slumped in bed, slobber on his chin, his fists balled, his eyes rolled back in his head. She comforted herself that Patsy had died in his sleep, but deep inside she knew better. She knew the bogies and the shadows had started fighting back, and that Patsy no longer had the courage to defend himself.

After she had grown used to him being dead, she lit a lamp in the kitchen and warmed water on the stove. She started by washing his heavy arms and his thick neck, then his barrel chest, his stomach, and the thighs from which all his great power had sprung. She kept on washing, and lied out loud to herself about him. She also lied about her own life, and that's what made her cry.

About all Patsy had left behind were the championship belt, a runaway son named Patsy, and a stack of debt that shamed Belty away from Colonel Harding and the circle of friends her husband's boxing had shaped for them. She gave up the rooms Patsy had let above a feed store on the river, and burrowed into a tarpaper "two by twice" in Smoky Hollow, a dog patch of rundown shacks on Smythe Street. Belty took in laundry and began selling apples on the street. And she wore the big brass buckle belt so people would know who she was.

The years spun out like wool. Her mind spun out with them. Belty had completely fallen inside herself. Some days she left her face in her hands from crying.

Belty got on like that for another ten years, and then her legs became so badly bowed she could hardly stand. A few churchgoers wrapped her in a grey cotton dress and imprisoned her in the Fredericton Home for the Poor, where the regime choked off her craziness and had her shivering at the sight of shadows.

The keepers took away her belt for her own protection, and with it they took away the outline of her soul. They left her with little to dream about, and nothing to do but finger the wrinkles on her own face and wait for the saggy weight of death to hang on her lips. She was seventy-two when she died in 1904. They buried her in a common grave in the poorhouse burying ground—buried her in the grey cotton dress, and without the big brass buckle belt that had set her apart from everyone else and given her the name "Belty."

LADY BANNERMAN

Margaret Gordon grew up in Charlottetown, Prince Edward Island. She was both pretty and brilliant, with a keen eye for what was fashionable. In 1810, when she was twelve, her father went bankrupt. He saw no way to satisfy his creditors in Charlottetown, and so packed off his family for Halifax. There his luck was even worse. Again, with his creditors close behind, he had the family on the move, this time to Aberdeen, Scotland, where he planned to sell family property to pay his debts.

Margaret, the youngest of the Gordon clan, was left with her aunt in Kirkcaldy, Scotland, while her father and family continued on to Aberdeen. In Kirkcaldy, a few years later, Margaret met Thomas Carlyle. He was just a lowly schoolmaster then, but destined to become one of the world's greatest scholars, writers, and social philosophers.

Margaret and Thomas fell in love and talked of marriage. But when the aunt heard such talk, she quickly interfered. She wanted someone of higher rank for Margaret, not a schoolmaster.

Thomas Carlyle honoured the aunt's wishes and withdrew from any further courting. But he never forgot, and often wrote about his first love—Margaret Gordon of Prince Edward Island.

There were many other suitors for Margaret's hand over the next few years, and one of them, Alexander Bannerman, won her heart. Alexander was an aristocrat, and through their marriage, Margaret became Lady Bannerman.

Her husband soon became governor of Prince Edward Island, and so Margaret Gordon returned to her island home as first lady. She reigned in Charlottetown, queen of Island society until 1854. She was fashionable and remarkably witty. She conversed with politicians, corresponded with poets, and discussed life and social philosophy with some of the leading thinkers of the day.

Henry Wadsworth Longfellow was said to remark upon meeting her: "We have no such woman in the United States as Lady Bannerman."

SPEED SKATER

There was nothing fancy about how he ice-skated, but my lord, he was fast!

Hugh McCormick was a New Brunswick farm boy who liked nothing better than ice-skating on the Kennebecasis River as fast as he could go. He practiced skating against the wind to build his endurance and to strengthen those driving muscles in his legs.

In the 1870s, Hugh went to a nearby blacksmith with a hand-drawn sketch of a skate blade. It was about nineteen inches long. The blacksmith said the blade looked like that section of the St. John River called Long Reach. From then on, Hugh McCormick referred to his oversized blades as Long Reach Speed Skates.

The comical look of those boat-shaped blades had spectators laughing—but not for long. As soon as Hugh McCormick laced on his skates, it seemed there was more blow to the wind, because when that boy skated past, he brought a rush behind him that could darn near straighten the curl in a young girl's head of hair.

Hugh McCormick became famous in New York and Minneapolis, the speed skating capitals of North America. And in 1882, the New Brunswick farm boy drove his Long Reach skates into the ice and defeated the world speed skating champion, Norway's Alex Paulsen.

Hugh McCormick remained world speed skating champion until 1893, when he lost the title to Fred Breen. Breen also grew up along the Kennebecasis River, not far from where Hugh McCormick had lived, and he just happened to be wearing a pair of Long Reach Speed Skates.

JACK ORMISTON

Jack Ormiston was built like a nail—thin, straight, and hard. He hunted and trapped the Cape Breton countryside in the 1890s. He was a man at home in the woods: he was shy, quiet, and most often avoided towns, people, and conversation. His jaws worked a chew of tobacco better than they did a mouthful of words. But every now and again Jack had a story to tell; like the one about the winter he tried crossing the Northeast Margaree River on a log.

He was about halfway across, carrying a can of kerosene and spilling some on his boots, when the log rolled and one oil-slick boot completely submerged and filled. He jerked and swung his weight to bring the log right, but the other boot went under too.

Now, it was cold! So cold that before he reached the riverbank, the water in his boots had frozen. He started walking to a farmhouse about five miles distant. He'd gone about a mile when he remembered the kerosene oil he carried.

He poured half in one boot and the rest in the other. Almost at once he could feel the kerosene thaw his feet and the ice inside his boots.

He walked another mile, and then even the kerosene oil began to freeze. Now Jack was desperate. He pulled matches from his pocket, lit one, and dropped it into his left boot. The kerosene oil caught fire and burned down to his canvas pants tucked inside. It thawed his foot, and when Jack felt his toes, he stomped out the fire. He set another fire inside his right boot, and let it burn until he felt his toes. Then he picked up his backpack and walked on to that farmhouse in time for supper.

Jack told his story, and the farmer had to see for himself. The insides of Jack's boots were scorched blacker than a farmer's field after spring burning. And his legs—why, his legs hardly had the hair singed.

Another story Jack liked to tell was about the time he wandered out of a hunting camp to be alone for a bit, to give himself a chance to think and feel the blanket comfort of the woods he loved so much.

While walking, he came across a bear climbing down out of a tree. One quick look, and Jack had that bear's hide sized and valued at thirty dollars. Jack had left his rifle at camp, but he wasn't about to let thirty dollars get away that easy.

He ran to the base of the tree and let loose one swift kick at that bear's rump, and that immediately stopped the bear's descent. Then Jack let out a wild yell for his partner, Jim Hodges, to come running. Jack kicked and yelled, kicked and yelled. He kicked so much, his right leg felt loaded with lead.

As Jack would tell it, he kicked himself into exhaustion. "I had 'bout one kick left, and then that old bear would be getting even. So I swung kick number forty-nine and flopped onto my back with the bear falling on top, about as dead as dead."

Jack said he kicked that bear to death, but Jim Hodges told it a different way, and always patted his rifle to make sure the listener got his meaning.

BALLEEN TAPESTRIES

While Alexander Graham Bell tinkered in Baddeck, Nova Scotia, with inventions that would revolutionize Western society, three sisters, not far away at Arichat, steadfastly practised their needlepoint. They were the Balleen sisters—Ida Maria, Margaret, and Louise. Little did they know their needlepoint would receive the world's attention.

At the time, there were only two examples of tapestry work done with needlepoint. One hung in the National Art Gallery in Dresden, Germany. The other hung in a church hall in Arichat.

The sisters came by their art quite accidentally, almost by a trick of fate.

They were shy and home-loving women, dedicated to one another. They had never married. The long winter nights had them occupying their time with needlepoint. On one occasion, one of the sisters discovered a famous painting depicted in the *London Illustrated News*. She decided to interpret the four-by-six-inch illustration into a four-by-eight-foot tapestry.

The other sisters did the same, working on separate tapestries and referencing different illustrations from the same source.

The tapestries took three years to complete, and as fate would have it, almost at once the fame of the Balleen sisters spread worldwide. Their tapestries went on exhibit throughout Europe, Australia, and the United States. In 1935, a Balleen tapestry was worth more than fifty thousand dollars.

Yet fate had another trick to play on the sisters. Because of the tightly focused work their needlepoint demanded and because of their intense dedication to perfection, all three of the Balleen sisters went blind.

RADCLIFF THE HANGMAN

A thick-set, good-looking man with a long, sandy moustache swung off the train in Moncton, New Brunswick. He wore a black broadcloth suit cut in the Prince Albert style. A conductor handed down his two black bags. One contained a change of clothes; the other held a black hood and a length of rope with a noose at one end.

The man was known as Radcliff, Canada's official hangman. And he had come to Moncton on business. The business he was about was the hanging of a cop killer named Buck Owen.

Word spread that Radcliff was in town, and a local reporter hung around the hotel lobby to get an interview. It was one of the few interviews Radcliff ever gave.

The first question was a natural, and Radcliff answered it without hesitation. He twirled an end of his sandy moustache as he spoke. He said he had become a hangman out of kindness.

One evening, Radcliff explained, he had read about a man suffering for fourteen minutes during a hanging in Ontario.

Radcliff had crumpled the newspaper, tossed it into the fire, and told his wife straight out that he could do a better job. And so he did.

Radcliff told the reporter that his first hanging was a murderer named Buchell, who had walked to the gallows as if going across the town square to get a drink. Radcliff hanged him clean and quick. Then there was LaMontaigne, a Quebec murderer who broke down and had to be carried to the gallows. During the excitement, and perhaps from the effort of lugging LaMontaigne up the platform steps, the sheriff took a heart attack and died. That created more commotion on the gallows. At last Radcliff had quieted the condemned man by assuring him that he would hardly feel a thing.

And then there was another fellow, who threw his wife over Niagara Falls. Radcliff allowed the man to kick off his boots because the condemned man wished not to die with them on.

On November 29, 1893, at 10:15 AM, Buck Owen walked through Dorchester prison yard with Father Cormier at his side. There were fifty witnesses, and Buck Owen shook their hands and asked them to pray for his soul. He then climbed the gallows to the hymn-singing of Mrs. Atkinson and Mrs. Emmerson. He greeted Radcliff with a nod. Radcliff slipped on the noose and the black hood. Buck said: "Let 'er go!"

The weight dropped. Buck shot up and came down with a jerk. He made a few twitches and was dead. It took all of three seconds.

SMALLPOX AND GRANNY ROSS

Smallpox inoculation dates back to the eighth century in India. There they used a small amount of a weakened or dead form of the pathogen, often obtained from the scabs of a smallpox victim, and purposely infected a healthy person to confer immunity. The Chinese adapted the practice a couple hundred years after, and by 1741 had refined the procedure and method of preserving smallpox scabs:

"Wrap the scabs carefully in paper and put them into a small container bottle. Cork it tightly so that the activity is not dissipated. The container must not be exposed to sunlight or warmed beside a fire. It is best to carry it for some time on the person so that the scabs dry naturally and slowly. The container should be marked clearly with the date on which the contents were taken from the patient."

The first inoculation for smallpox in North America took place in 1721 during an outbreak of the dreaded disease. Cotton Mather, a Boston minister, heard about this practice from one of his African slaves and suggested that Zabdiel Boylston, a doctor, try it out on a couple of Mather's slaves and on Mather's son. Boylston did, and later inoculated three hundred others in the community.

It worked. Only six of the inoculated died, while the mortality rate of the un-inoculated was one in six.

Boylston published the results in London in 1724, but it took decades before inoculation became common practice. In fact, people feared inoculation, and some threatened those who favoured it.

In 1777, during a smallpox outbreak in Nova Scotia, the townsfolk of Horton severely beat two men for inoculating themselves and their families.

Those in neighbouring Windsor, however, took a different view. They welcomed the old woman who came with "a nutshell full of matter of the best sort of smallpox." The old woman would ask what vein a person wanted to use. "She then rips open that which you offer her and puts into it as much venom as can lie upon the end of a needle."

In the 1860s, a smallpox epidemic broke out in The Forks, a community in the Margaree Valley in Cape Breton. There was not a doctor to be had for more than a hundred miles. One case became two, and two became a dozen. People feared their whole community would be devastated.

That's when Thomas Ross remembered all the old stories his great-granny had told him. Granny Ross had died in 1860, after living for 110 years. For most of her life she had doctored Margaree families for miles around. She had lived through a smallpox epidemic herself, and had cared for the dying with a smallpox vaccine. She had often told her grandchildren and great-grandchildren about how she drew vaccine from one of her patients and had saved it in a small wooden box all these years.

Thomas Ross remembered that story, and found the vaccine just where his granny had said it would be—in a small wooden box on a shelf in an old cupboard. Granny Ross had carefully preserved it between glass that was sealed with spruce gum and rolled in wax.

Thomas Ross went door to door with the vaccine. People vaccinated each other and waited...and waited...and waited. Some had their doubts and feared for their lives. After all, Granny Ross's vaccine was more than seventy years old. But it worked. It stopped the spread of smallpox in the Margaree Valley and saved the lives of nearly a hundred families.

LIGHTHOUSE KEEPER

John Boyd, the lighthouse keeper at Spruce Point, near St. Stephen, New Brunswick, took a short turn away from home that fall of 1882. He left the lighthouse in the joint care of his wife, Kate, and his eldest daughter. The daughter's name was Roberta Grace.

On the night of October 8, a storm blew in off the Passamaquoddy Bay. Over the wind and thunder, Roberta heard the high-pitched cries of desperate men. She threw on a heavy coat and, against her mother's warning, dragged a twelve-foot open boat from the beach and launched it into the St. Croix River.

With back-breaking strokes, she forced that boat through the angry water until she saw the outline of an overturned sailboat. She manoeuvred her boat around the dangerous clutter of sails and rigging. And then she saw the faces of four trapped and drowning men.

It took every ounce of her strength to steady her boat and drag the men up over the side. And it was not until they reached shore that the men realized their rescuer was a twenty-one-year-old woman.

Roberta never said a word about that night in 1882, but the men did. They told everyone they met about the courage of that girl at Spruce Point, New Brunswick, and how they would not be alive had it not been for her.

The following year, the government of Canada presented her with a gold watch with the inscription: "To Roberta Grace Boyd, in recognition of her humane exertions in saving life in the St. Croix River on the 8th of October, 1882."

JOHN FEINDEL, A SOLDIER AT VIMY RIDGE

In April 1917, Canadian forces attacked three divisions of the German Sixth Army at Vimy Ridge in the Nord-Pas-de-Calais region of France. There was probably no fiercer fight during World War One. Losses were heavy.

The day before the attack, John Feindel, an Annapolis Valley, Nova Scotia, boy who had recently dropped out of Acadia University to join the war effort, wrote this in his diary:

> April 16th, 1917. This morning General MacDonald gave us a speech and pointed out how highly efficient the Canadian Corps was thought of by General Headquarters. Then he told us we had been chosen to take Vimy Ridge, the key to the Western Front. Vimy Ridge is part of the Hindenburg Line and well protected.
>
> The General said that if we take Vimy Ridge Canadian arms will be world famous for ever in history.
>
> This evening we heard that Zero Hour has been set back 24 hours. I expect it will be a hard job and we will no doubt have heavy casualties. But it must be done for Canada, our native country, which means home and loved ones and all we hold dear.
>
> I have been fortunate this year in many ways. The ones at home have not forgotten me in their prayers.
>
> If I am spared, I hope I will be able to do something worthwhile. If I am not spared, I cannot help that."

That was John Feindel's last diary entry. The following morning, Canadian forces attacked and captured Vimy Ridge, and John Feindel was killed.

THE NEW BRUNSWICK STRONGMAN

(BJG)

New Brunswick has had its share of mythical strongmen. But in the 1930s, central New Brunswick had one strongman whose feats were real.

Ira Gosman, a six-foot, three-hundred-pound woodsman from Marysville, near Fredericton, spent most of his working life on the Miramichi and Nashwaak Rivers. His physical powers were legendary. His fellow woodsmen often watched in wonder to see him pack a barrel of pork up on his shoulder, and carry it from a supply scow up a steep riverbank to the cookhouse.

Once, when he was suspected of committing some misdemeanour, Gosman hid from authorities under a sloven wagon. Such a wagon was heavy enough to need at least four good men to lift it. While hiding, it came on to rain, and when his pursuers gave up the chase, Gosman swung around, lifted the wagon on his shoulders, and used it as an umbrella to get to his destination.

One year, the strongman was part of a crew driving timber on the Southwest Miramichi when a smart aleck from Fredericton insulted him. Ira Gosman was a black man, and the arrogant young man said to him, "And how come they brought you along?"—meaning, why was a black man working with a white crew?

Gosman said nothing.

A day or two later, the young wit slipped into the water between the floating logs, and was within moments of drowning. Gosman swept his great arm down, pulled his tormentor from the icy waters, and stood him on the safety of the raft.

"There!" said Gosman. "That's why they brought me along."

MARY EARLY—WITCH

Mary Early was a witch. Not the devil-worshipping kind, but a woman who knew natural cures and remedies, concocted love potions, and read a person's dreams.

It was said that Mary Early was in competition with the medical profession in Halifax, and that she had the better record. She certainly had a sizable clientele, and many of them were wealthy and well-to-do. They were loyal, too.

On November 25, 1826, William Figgins of Dartmouth finally took his wife's advice about curing the ulcer he had been suffering for the past year. He crossed the harbour by ferry and visited Mary Early's one-room shack in the north end of Halifax. It was a dimly lit room cluttered with jars, barrels, and crocks containing animal paws, teeth, ears, and innards. She also stocked huge tubs of fermenting berries. She mixed a concoction of pungent root, pine oil, and juniper with a pint of water, boiled it down to a half pint, and served it to William Figgins.

An hour later, Figgins was on his way home when he felt a great heat in his stomach and "a strangeness" in his head, as though he were about to fly into the air and burst. Frightened, he stopped at Doctor Avery's drugstore on Portland Street in Dartmouth, explained what ailed him, and then dropped stone cold dead.

Doctor Wallace, the coroner, listened to Doc Avery's testimony and ruled that Figgins had died from Mary's concoction. The following month, Mary faced trial for murder.

At her trial, Mary argued that Figgins came to her on his own and drank by his own consent, and that his ulcer was so far gone he would have died anyway. The jury, some of Mary's regular customers, believed Mary Early the witch and not Doctor Wallace the coroner. The verdict: Not guilty!

WILLIAM ROSS

The Nova Scotia Fencibles had earned the land grants they received in Nova Scotia's Annapolis and Cornwallis valleys by fighting well during the Napoleonic War in Europe, and against the Americans during the War of 1812. Now, in 1816, under the command of Captain William Ross, the entire company and their families boarded a transport ship, the *Archduke Charles*, and sailed from Quebec for Nova Scotia.

The transport sailed the Gulf of St. Lawrence, rounded Cape Breton Island, and navigated the ragged and island-strewn eastern coast for Halifax. Near Jeddore, the ship struck a submerged rock. The sea rushed into the gaping hole, and the ship listed in about fifteen feet of water.

Soldiers and their families clung to the gunwales while breakers battered the ship into a splintered wreck. Hope was running out.

Captain Ross grabbed one end of a towrope and dove into the pounding sea. He washed up on shore with the rope still in hand. He secured it to a boulder and ordered his strongest men to guide one passenger at a time along the grab-line to safety.

Only six passengers perished. The rest made it to Halifax, and eventually to their land grants between the Annapolis Valley and Nova Scotia's South Shore. They named the new settlement after their brave leader—New Ross.

COLBERT'S WAKE

John Colbert was a Halifax butcher, an amiable, well-liked man. In 1862, something snapped in John's head. He was committed to the poor and insane asylum in Halifax where, on April 16, he committed suicide.

Elizabeth Colbert, John's wife, claimed the body and removed it to her house on Proctor's Lane for a wake and funeral. Dozens of friends and relatives gathered at the Colbert house to pay their respects. Pretty soon it was time for the mourners to close the coffin and march the body to the graveyard for burial.

Just then the front door banged open and Edward Jennings, the coroner, entered with two medical students close behind. Without a word to the wife of the deceased, he marched straight to the coffin, threw open the lid, removed the death shroud, and proceeded to perform an autopsy. He made a deep incision in the dead man's throat and removed the windpipe. He then held it up to public scrutiny and gave the medical students an anatomy lesson.

The mourners stood horrified, then some broke into wild hysteria. An older woman fainted. Elizabeth convulsed with sobs. She begged Jennings to stop, but the coroner ignored her plea, opening the dead man's chest and examining the heart.

With the autopsy complete, Jennings sewed up the body and departed as boldly as he had entered.

Weeks later, Jennings defended his actions before a judge on the grounds that a suicide required an autopsy. The judge agreed, dismissed Liz Colbert's suit, and advised Jennings: "In future, man, choose a more suitable time and place for dissection."

BILL WHELPLEY

Bill Whelpley was an ice skater from Saint John, New Brunswick, a barrel-chested boy with legs as thick as tree trunks.

Bill liked to race on the ice on the St. John River; and he liked to race for money—but not your nickel-and-dime hundred-yard dashes. A race of under five miles was not for Bill Whelpley. He raced for speed and endurance. And in the 1890s, he was the best in the world.

Bill Whelpley held the world record for ice races over five miles. He raced anyone and everyone. He travelled Canada, the United States, and Europe, taking on all challengers. He always bet a hundred on himself, then skated five 5-mile races one after the other, non-stop. And he never lost a single race.

In 1893, a New York man laid two thousand dollars on a table with an open challenge to Bill Whelpley—ten hours of continuous skating, and the skater who travels the furthest wins. Bill took the bet.

Ten hours later, Bill was 117 miles distant, while the New York challenger had skated only 72 miles.

Bill was so confident of his endurance and skating ability that he offered five hundred dollars to any man in the world who could beat him in an ice-skating race of over fifty miles. There were plenty of takers, but nobody beat Bill Whelpley.

It was not until the 1930s, when Bill was an old man, that someone beat him in a five-mile race—and then just barely.

Plain and Simple

HOLEY DOLLARS

Maritimers once did a lot of business in the Caribbean Islands and South America. These were Spanish colonies in the eighteenth century, and they traded in Spanish dollars. As money changed hands, Spanish dollars became common and valuable currency in Nova Scotia and Prince Edward Island. However, their value varied from province to province. In Halifax, a Spanish dollar was worth eight shillings, while in PEI its value was six.

Island merchants tended to hoard these Spanish dollars and later trade them in Halifax for the higher exchange rate. This soon produced a scarcity of coin on PEI, and that led to some economic hardship.

In 1815, Governor Charles Douglas Smith got the bright idea to round up the Spanish dollars on the Island and punch out the centre, making two coins of lesser value. He had them re-stamped with a sunburst. He valued the silver in the punched-out centre at one shilling, and that in the outer rim at about five shillings.

It turned out just as Governor Smith had expected. Few merchants outside of PEI wanted these "holey dollars," as they came to be called, and that meant the currency remained on the Island.

Then a shopkeeper at Caledonia, PEI, discovered that the silver in the punched-out centre weighed a shilling more than Governor Smith had said the coin was worth. This shopkeeper bought up all the punched-out centres he could find, until he had a large chest full of them. Then he shipped the chest to England for the coins to be melted and sold for the silver. He thought he would make a killing. He didn't.

On its way to England, the ship sank.

CLAN LOYALTY

During times of war, we tend to believe the other side engages in barbarisms that our boys would shun. Our side is always on the side of "right," and behaves accordingly. The enemy is always in the wrong. They are brutes, sporting horns and pointed tails.

During the War of 1812, Donald Shaw ran a cargo vessel out of Charlottetown, Prince Edward Island, and regularly braved the threat of American privateers. A privateer was a privately owned warship commissioned by its respective government to prey on enemy shipping. The Maritime provinces had their fair share of privateers, and so did the Americans.

Most PEI, New Brunswick, and Nova Scotia sailors believed the waterfront talk that sailors aboard the American privateers, unlike the sailors aboard their own, behaved like pirates and would sooner kill a captured crew as ransom them.

On June 16, 1812, Donald Shaw raised telescope and saw the square sails and flag of an American privateer. The coaster's crew battened the cargo and made a run for shallow water, but the American vessel was trim and fast, and its sails seemed to grow as it closed on the coastal boat.

Within a few hours, the privateer drew within fifty yards of Donald Shaw's cargo ship and fired a cannonball across her bow. Shaw had no choice but to hove to and take his chances with surrender.

As the Americans boarded with pistols drawn and knives gleaming in the bright sun, Shaw and his crew feared for their lives. Then the American captain swung aboard the coaster and boldly claimed the captured ship as a prize of war, along with its cargo and valuables.

Donald Shaw heard a Scottish lilt in the American's voice. Shaw, himself a highlander, answered in Gaelic, and the American captain replied in the same highland tongue.

"The Isle of Mull," Shaw said, and held out his hand.

"The Isle of Mull myself," the American replied, and lowered his pistol.

On that heaving sea, with war raging between their two countries and feelings running deep with animosity, these two highlanders sat down on deck for an hour or more, laughing together as they recalled their boyhoods in the same highland village. And later they parted friends, because clan loyalty proved stronger than the bad blood of war and the irrational fear of the enemy.

However, friendship did not contravene the rules of a privateer, and so the American captain kept the coaster boat and its cargo, which he would later sell in Boston upon his return.

BASEBALL'S BEGINNINGS

In that first official baseball game on July 27, 1867, it was the Halifax Baseball Club against the Halifax Independents. Before the teams could play ball, the players had to clear the field of the cows and sheep grazing on the Commons, and then map out a diamond. Rolled-up coats and cow flops served as bases, a tapered stick as a bat, and a sawdust-packed pig's ear as a ball.

Flump! The batter walloped the first pitch, and baseball in the Maritimes was officially underway. That first game was the furthest thing from a pitcher's duel. The final score was seventy-seven to fifty-five in favour of the Halifax Club. But the Independents got their revenge in the rematch scheduled for September 7, 1867.

During the interval, the Halifax Independents searched for a better "ball tosser" than the one they had. The team found him in a tavern, three sheets to the wind and with his cap to starboard. His name was Henry Keeling, and he was the best-known pitcher when sober—second-best when drunk.

Throughout the night of September 6, the Independents guarded Keeling from the demon rum, and on game day, Keeling was in top form. He whirled like a windmill before throwing the ball, then served up fastballs so fast batters thought he was throwing cod eyes. Keeling was a showboat. He strutted about the mound with each out, and screwed up his face in anger at the opposition with each hit.

The fans loved it. Henry "Shakes" Keeling was masterful, and behind his sober pitching, the Halifax Independents defeated the Halifax Baseball Club thirty-three to twenty-eight.

That was the start of it. The baseball bug bit deep, and Maritime men and women have been playing the game ever since.

COST OF MARRIAGE

Colonel Gay was a Loyalist who had settled at Fort Cumberland, Nova Scotia, near Amherst, shortly after the American Revolution. He was a tall, barrel-chested man whose mere presence in a room commanded attention. He was also the local magistrate. As such, he earned his living from the fees he received for looking after the community's civil affairs—such as wills, deeds, marriages, and divorces.

One day in 1790, Colonel Gay was in an upstairs room shaving when he overheard two servants, Julius and Dianna, cooing and whispering about getting married. The colonel poked his head from the window and told the couple, if they were fixed on marriage, he would arrange the certificate and perform the ceremony right after breakfast. But it would cost them, the colonel said, about two dollars.

Neither servant had the two dollars, but Dianna had a lace napkin that she quickly sold for the cost of getting married. Later that morning, the colonel married them and collected his fee.

About a month later, Colonel Gay again heard Julius and Dianna beneath his window. This time they were arguing. The colonel met with them straight away, and listened as both sides told their sad story of married life.

Julius said every day it was fight, fight, fight. He firmly wanted to be unmarried.

Dianna was more practical than that. She just wanted her two dollars back. She told the colonel the goods she bought "wasn't worth the price."

The colonel smiled and told the couple that divorce would cost them double what they had paid to be married.

Julius and Dianna shrugged and scowled and kicked at the dirt on their way home. The high cost of divorce encouraged them to make the most of what they had originally bargained for.

BIG CITY

(BJG)

With high-speed jet travel, most Maritimers think nothing about the hop, skip, and jump to Florida for an eye-opening visit to Disney World, or to Mexico, or Costa Rica, or across Canada to Vancouver. The world has become such a small place that it is downright easy to take our own backyard for granted.

In earlier times, it was common for rural Maritimers to spend an entire lifetime without ever travelling beyond the county in which they were born. For such persons, excursions into the big city were awe-inspiring.

In 1909, the *Saint John Standard* reported that a Fredericton visitor, George Gibson, had been arrested. Gibson, the paper said, "became bewildered on looking at the tall buildings of Saint John and lost himself..." He bumped and banged pedestrians, and darn near killed himself under a delivery wagon. Police arrested him for his own safety, and a magistrate told him to go home.

A year later, the same paper reported the death and burial of Mrs. William Nelson, then seventy-six. She belonged at Summer Hill, a settlement in backcountry Queens County, New Brunswick—now swallowed up by Canadian Forces Base Gagetown.

She, too, visited the big city—just once.

The paper says: "...she had not seen a railway train, steamboat, or street car until about six years ago, when she visited Saint John—and at that time the unwonted excitement had such a powerful effect that she had been mentally unbalanced until her death."

And that was Saint John. Imagine if those country folk had seen New York, London, or Par-ee!

UNWANTED EMPLOYMENT

Captain Thomas Mellish, provost marshal of Prince Edward Island, advertised a large sum of money to the person who would perform a particular criminal execution. There were no takers. On its own, the hangman's job was bad enough, but in this instance, during the winter of 1778, it was doubly so. The condemned thief was a woman, who history records only by the name of Mary.

Even though Mary was an old offender, running up charges for drunkenness and assault, and now this, her second charge for robbery, she was still a woman. And no God-fearing man on the Island wanted to be known for taking a woman to dance on nothing.

Thomas Mellish suggested that the hanging be postponed until the ice left the Northumberland Strait and a hangman could be brought to Nova Scotia. The acting governor said no. He ordered Mellish to find another man to hang the woman, or Mellish would have to hang her himself.

Thomas Mellish brooded over his options. An hour passed, then another. At last, he hunched over his writing desk and wrote his resignation as provost marshal. Since no one else would take Mellish's vacant position, the execution of justice now fell at the feet of the acting governor.

With public opinion now rallying against him, and with the responsibility for hanging Mary the thief weighing heavy on his mind, the acting governor rose from bed in the small hours of February 3, 1778, and issued orders for the condemned woman's immediate release.

SLOAT'S CANNON

Sloat's Slough is a small swamp on the east side of the St. John River, about nine miles above Fredericton, New Brunswick. Several decades ago, the owner was the widow of George Sloat.

For two and a half centuries, there lingered a legend that a French cannon lay at the bottom of Sloat's Slough, and in 1929, when a freak weather system froze the river at the lowest level anyone could remember, a local antique collector, Charles Duplessis, resolved to find the lost gun.

He made a sharpened steel pole, and, patiently plunging it into the half-frozen mud, probed the slough till he hit metal. Here he dug, and came up with the missing cannon. It was more of a brass swivel gun, with a three-foot barrel that fired small shot and scrap metal.

It was indeed a French-made gun, and it probably once served the French fort at Jemseg. A Dutch adventurer pillaged Jemseg in 1674, and the French, to escape their pursuer, fled upriver, and probably threw the gun into the slough to prevent its capture.

No sooner did Charles Duplessis land the cannon than the widow Sloat sued him for ownership. The widow won the suit, then quickly sold the cannon to the New Brunswick government for one thousand dollars. The province thought it would make a fine addition to the New Brunswick museum in Saint John.

But somehow the cannon never made it that far. Someone lost it, or sold it, or simply kept it for his or her private collection. However it was, that French swivel cannon, buried in Sloat's Slough for two and a half centuries, had disappeared again.

BORN LOSER

On the night of July 30, 1814, Francis Keonig, a private in the 60th Regiment stationed in Halifax, tossed back another beer and continued telling the tale of his luckless life. His drinking companion was a bugler boy by the name of Adrian DeBohn. It seems bad luck had followed Keonig since the day he marked his "X" and took the king's shilling to join the British Army. He feared going into battle, believing that with his bad luck, he would be the first to take a musket ball between the eyes.

The bugler listened dutifully, the price he paid for the beer Keonig bought.

Just then the door to the public house banged open, and Private Fenneback staggered in, drunk and belligerent. He pointed at the bugler and ordered the boy to leave. Fennenback was particular about who drank with him, and a young, whey-faced bugler was not to his liking.

Keonig insisted the bugler stay. Fenneback slapped Keonig, and Keonig returned the blow. Then Fenneback challenged, and Keonig accepted, a duel behind the South Barracks.

A torch was their only light. The bugler held the weapons under his arms with only the handles showing. Fenneback tossed a halfpenny coin for choice of weapons.

Keonig called it right and made his choice, drawing a twelve-inch knife from under the bugler's arm. Fenneback then withdrew a sword three times longer than Keonig's knife.

Keonig hardly defended himself. It was as though he recognized his luckless choice of weapon as simply the last act in a luckless life.

Fenneback had only to make one thrust, and Keonig was dead.

THIRSTY INGENUITY

(BJG)

The Canada Temperance Act—better known as the Scott Act—made it illegal to sell booze in Canada in the 1920s. There was a strong lobby of prohibitionists who got the act passed. But the thing these prohibitionists did not reckon on was the ingenuity of the thirsty.

Lincoln is a community in Sunbury County, New Brunswick, almost on Fredericton's doorstep. There, one day in 1928, provincial police discovered a huge cache of smuggled booze hidden under a barn. The stuff had to go to police headquarters in Fredericton for disposal. According to the Temperance Act, the police had to pour off any liquor they seized in a raid.

At police headquarters in Fredericton, a senior officer checked off the amount reported seized, then kept a careful eye on the "demon rum" as junior men poured it down a sink.

There was a catch, however.

Headquarters was on the second floor of a building directly over a York Street hardware store, and the sink's drainpipe ran down through the store beneath.

News of the haul spread like a firestorm. When the police were read to pour the liquor off, there were also on hand a host of clerks, their friends, customers, and almost anyone who could lay hands on a bucket, pan, Mason jar—anything that would hold liquid.

Hardware stores have lots of hacksaws. And with that cut pipe pulled a few inches to one side, hardly a drop of rum went to waste in the city sewers.

Against such ingenuity, the forces of Temperance in the Maritimes never had a chance.

SUNDAY BOATING

(BJG)

The first highway bridge across the St. John River at Fredericton was built in 1886. Before that, folks rowed across or took the ferry. But even with the new bridge, there were still those who preferred taking their chances on the water to walking over it. Some were stubborn, others unwelcoming of change.

On the morning of Sunday, June 6, church-bound people on the new bridge stopped to watch an elderly man named Nearin and his wife making a dreadful botch of boating across the river. Mrs. Nearin wanted nothing to do with walking the new bridge, and she wouldn't let her husband use it either.

Nearin rowed first in one direction, then in another. His wife shouted orders, and Nearin followed them as best he could. All the while, their boat drifted closer to a guard pier.

When the elderly couple fought their way clear of the guard pier, it was plain they were incompetent—and in serious trouble.

Only one other boat was in the area at the time—a sailboat crewed by Fred and Louis Laforest. They made all haste to help the helpless.

Meanwhile, the Nearins' boat hit a bridge pier, upset, and left the old couple clinging to their overturned craft. Their cries for help rang strong at first, then grew fainter and fainter. The Laforests reached the couple with only seconds to spare. They landed the exhausted pair on the south shore. Here the Nearins sat till they recovered enough strength to walk and to talk.

And here, human nature soon took over.

The wife picked up right where she had left off—blaming her husband for the mishap. The last the churchgoers on the bridge heard was Mrs. Nearin's voice (much the louder) bewailing the loss of her summer hat and vowing she'd give up churchgoing if it meant "walking 'cross that bridge."

SMALLPOX VACCINATION

(BJG)

Compulsory vaccination against smallpox for all New Brunswick children went on the law books in 1902. Outbreaks of the dread disease took place from time to time in the years following, among those old enough to have missed the nurse's visits to public schools.

When one of these local epidemics hit Saint John in 1918, the Board of Health ordered all the unvaccinated to visit their doctors for a shot. Most complied—even the squeamish who feared scratches and hypo needles.

But every crowd has its share of smart alecks, and a Saint John newspaper, the *Standard*, reported on one of these—a young man whose name it omitted.

Accompanied by a friend, this lad visited his doctor and received the scratch, and the doctor applied the vaccine. Then as soon as the doctor's back was turned, the fellow wiped the vaccine off with his handkerchief. As the pair left the doctor's office, the boy told his friend what he had done. "You can bet I wasn't going to have a sore arm," he said.

Moments later, and forgetting he had a popped pimple on his nose, he wiped it with the same handkerchief. You can guess the rest.

In a couple days, his nose grew sore, reddened, and, as the newspaper says, swelled so much that the young fellow "became almost cross-eyed looking at it."

It wasn't a landmark in medical history, just the only known case of a person getting a smallpox vaccination in the nose.

BUMBLING THIEVES

Thomas Hurley and Henry Funright were two down-on-their-luck Loyalists who did not share half a brain between them. Stealing was Hurley's idea.

In February 1789, they sat in Hurley's clapboard shack in Halifax, Nova Scotia, choking with smoke from a fire in a pit they had dug in the dirt floor. Their stomachs grumbled with hunger.

"We'll pinch a cow," Hurley said. "We'll walk out the Sackville Road and pinch a cow."

And so they did. They waited for the light snow to stop falling, then tracked out to Andrew Stewart's farm and stole his cow.

Funright thought the snow was a good thing, because they led the cow deep into the woods to butcher it, and as Funright said, "Our footprints in the snow will show us the way out."

Their footprints also showed Andrew Stewart and George Walters the way in. The silver filigree of the thieves' prints led from Stewart's barn straight to the spot where Hurley and Funright were up to their elbows in butchered beef.

The judge shook his head sadly when he was about to sentence Thomas Hurley and Henry Funright. He said out loud in court that such ninnies challenged his sense of justice. How could he possibly sentence these two bumbling thieves to the gallows? They were no more a threat to society than Geofrey Hogg, another thief who had stood before the bar only an hour before. Geofrey Hogg had been caught stealing by a blind man, who had heard the scrape of a coin being gently lifted from his money bowl.

The judge pitied these fools, and sentenced Hurley, Funright, and Hogg to transportation from Nova Scotia to Bermuda, where they could enjoy the gawk and blather of each other's company.

MARY WEBB

In Halifax, on a woolly morning in April 1758, a washerwoman named Anne Pentenny saw Mary Webb near Freshwater Brook, stomping down a mound of newly dug dirt. The washerwoman waited until Mary Webb had gone, then dug up what Mary had buried. She found an infant with the umbilical cord still attached.

A doctor examined the corpse and declared that the infant had been living at birth. It bore no marks of violence. The doctor later examined Mary Webb and declared that she had recently delivered a child.

Nathan Nathans and Sam Blayden, town magistrates, read the doctor's declaration and convened the grand jury to inquire into the infant's death. When they questioned Mary Webb, she broke into tears and confessed to squeezing life into a blood-swirled puddle between her legs and doing nothing to help it live.

Mary Webb was a maidservant, a floor scrubber, a gawky London girl who had been bedazzled by the recruiting agent's promise of a better life in Nova Scotia. Recruiting agents were known as "soul sellers," and they made a business of transshipping emigrants to businessmen and governments, which paid by the head for sorely needed labourers, servants, and settlers. Many of these immigrants came as indentured servants.

And so Mary Webb had indentured herself for the passage, traded her freedom for what she believed was opportunity. Once she arrived in Halifax, Nova Scotia, she learned otherwise.

In Nova Scotia, as in most of the colonies, an indentured servant was chattel, master owned and master ruled. A servant's life was hard work and no play. No love. No marriage. No chance to rub off the rut of youth—except upright in the woodshed, or in an alley, or in the woods outside the palisade with her skirts hitched and his breeches unbuttoned.

For unmarried indentured servants, fornication was outlawed. Not on moral grounds alone, but also because pregnancy was the inevitable result. The law was practical. Pregnancy meant lost work for the master, and lost work was a servant's violation of the indenture contract. That's why the law gave a master the right to punish servants caught fornicating by whipping them at the public whipping post. Twenty-one lashes. Sometimes thirty. The law deemed the public punishment a scourge for the wicked and a deterrent for those looking on.

Pregnancy had a punishment all its own, less harsh than the whipping post but more lasting. If a maidservant got herself with child, then the work lost during her pregnancy added time to the length of her indenture. The birth of a child also tacked on time. A child meant more cost for the master and less work from the mother. A master had the legal right to demand as much as two years' extra service for a bastard's birth. Pregnancy and childbirth often meant three more years of servitude. Three more years whittled from a woman's youth. Three years stacked with shame, and afterward stretched into a lifetime of hard work and poverty for the unmarried mother.

That's why pregnancy had Mary Webb sweating with fear for nine months, hiding the bulge, chewing sumac leaves to miscarry, and ravelling her nerves like yarn. Mary Webb came to term with a curse for motherhood and a foolishness to bury the ill-gotten child still wet with birth.

A murderer, Mary Webb, is what the jury said—twelve men, one verdict. "Mary Webb, the accused, is guilty of murdering a male infant born of her body."

And according to the law: "Any woman delivering a bastard child that she drowns or buries to hide its birth shall suffer death as in murder."

Chief Justice Jonathan Belcher agreed with the evidence and the jury's verdict. The evidence proved Mary Webb was a murderer, but what the evidence did not reveal was whether Mary Webb had killed her child willingly, or if the pain and trauma of childbirth had turned away her mind and heart from mothering her own child.

It was this doubt that had the chief justice delaying her execution and appealing to the Lords of Trade at the home office in England for permission to reprieve Mary Webb from the gallows.

There came no response from the Lords of Trade, not a word that it would even consider allowing a reprieve for this wretch of a woman. For four years, Mary Webb suffered in a stink-hole of a jail, rag-wrapped on a straw tick on a dirt floor, shivering in winter, wheezy from the hot stink in summer. Her fly-blown hair and skin crawled with scratch scabs and pock sores. Her insides hurt and her urine turned the colour of pus. For four years, she wished she had died the way she should have died—hanged for murdering the life she had given.

In March 1762, while still in jail, Mary Webb received her wish—she turned her face to the wall and, according to the coroner's report, died by "the visitation of God."

SMOKING

(BJG)

For nearly three hundred years, and as late as the 1930s, Maritime doctors prescribed tobacco smoke as a cure for asthma, insomnia, and certain intestinal discomforts.

On January 3, 1930, a Saint John newspaper ran a story about a boy who was keeping his New Year's resolution to stop smoking. His name was Billy Russell Howard, and for two years he had smoked a pipe daily. But now he was going to quit. Here's what the paper said:

"The family physician recommended a pipe to cure the child's insomnia. Then, Billy became a habitual smoker. The tobacco habit, however, made Billy a new man. Before smoking, he was sickly and seldom slept more than three or four hours at night. Now he is the very picture of health and the most active child in the neighbourhood."

After two whole years, Billy decided to kick the habit. He was well now, and not all that old. In fact, he had just turned three!

A month later, the same Saint John newspaper carried the story of another smoker—Elias White, who had lived all his life in Marysville (now part of Fredericton).

As of 1930, Elias still remembered vividly Fredericton's Great Fire of 1850, and Prince Albert Edward's visit in 1860. Elias said in an interview that he believed a life with hard work, no liquor, and lots of exercise "kept him in the good health he still enjoys."

At the age of ninety, Elias White admitted he'd smoked for seventy of those ninety years. His doctors had recommended it. And he said he didn't think it did him a bit of harm.

CHIGNECTO SHIP RAILWAY

The Chignecto Isthmus is a thin strip of land that connects Nova Scotia to the rest of Canada. Because of it, ships from the United States and western Nova Scotia have to sail all the way around

Nova Scotia to reach the Gulf of St. Lawrence. Even today, the trip is long and dangerous.

In the 1870s, Henry George Ketchum got the idea to build a ship railway across the Chignecto Isthmus. Ketchum was an engineer from Woodstock, New Brunswick. He had been the chief engineer on the São Paulo Railway in Brazil, and he built the railway between Amherst and Moncton. His idea for the Chignecto Ship Railway sounded simple: build a cradle in which ships could be lifted and placed on a flatbed railcar, then have them carried seventeen miles overland across the isthmus from Tidnish to Fort Lawrence.

Ketchum's plan would take a double line of tracks with extra-heavy rails. The cradle was to be 230 feet long and 40 feet wide. And the railway car was to have 192 wheels and travel at a speed of ten miles per hour. Ketchum's plan also called for excavating a basin on the Bay of Fundy side of the isthmus. It was to be 500 feet wide and 40 feet deep, and reinforced with masonry. It was a prodigious enterprise that was every bit as costly as it was ambitious.

Nevertheless, Ketchum's proposal caught the attention of Charles Tupper, then the federal minister of railroads and canals. With Tupper's encouragement, Ketchum incorporated the Chignecto Marine Transport Company in 1882, raised money in London, England, and in Ottawa, then rolled up his sleeves and got to work.

Henry Ketchum had three-quarters of the ship railway finished when, in 1890, he ran out of money. Work stopped and the project was abandoned.

Ketchum seemed to lose heart at the sight of his unfinished railway. His mood darkened and his days were anything but happy. He died in 1896, and lies buried in Tidnish, not far from the spot where he first dreamed of a railway to carry ships across the Chignecto Isthmus.

THE GOOD OF GOSSIP

Francis Flood, a journeyman carpenter in Halifax and a bit of a ladies' man, married a pretty servant girl in June 1826. They were hardly two days wed when a rumour spread door to door, at last reaching the ears of young Mrs. Flood.

According to the rumour, Francis Flood was already married to an Irish girl, who had recently arrived in Halifax on the ship *Rubicon* and was now searching the town for Francis Flood.

The new Mrs. Flood hung her head and wept that she had married Francis Flood against all warnings about his philandering ways. Then she plucked up her courage and marched to where Francis was building a house on Queen Street. She confronted him face to face, declaring for all within earshot that she was off to the bishop to have their marriage pronounced null and void, and then to a magistrate to have him arrested for bigamy.

Francis denied the accusation and begged his wife for time to set the matter right. Mrs. Flood granted him two hours. Francis dashed to the waterfront and then around the town, like a dog chasing deer. When the two hours were nearly gone, he burst through the door of their small apartment with the *Rubicon*'s passenger list in hand and six witnesses in tow.

The Irish girl's name was not on the list, and the witnesses swore that the rumour was a joke started by the best man, who by this time had given the story to the *Novascotian* newspaper.

For many years after, laughter followed young Mrs. Flood wherever she went. But she bore it all very well. After all, the laughs and snickers helped keep Francis home at night, a devoted and very dutiful husband.

SCHOOLTEACHERS

In 1906, a female teacher in Nova Scotia earned less than three hundred dollars for a school year. That was not a lot of money even then, and teachers did a whole lot more than teach. Most had to scrub and clean the one-room schoolhouse from floor to ceiling. Their value as teachers was not only measured against how well their students learned, but also against their housekeeping abilities.

In that year, School Inspector Bruce of Yarmouth and Shelburne counties announced that he would be travelling his circuit, inspecting the schools and evaluating the teaching staff. Such an announcement typically gave teachers time to spruce up their classrooms and coach students through the usual run of questions an inspector might ask.

But that year, instead of travelling by horse and buggy, Inspector Bruce took the train. And that had him on the doorsteps of the county schools days, and sometimes weeks, before expected.

He found un-swept classrooms dirty with litter and gravel, and he marvelled that "a young woman raised in a clean home could be content to live in such filth."

Unprepared pupils demonstrated poor reading skills and little knowledge of English grammar. Their spelling was careless, and their arithmetic even worse. As for their singing, Inspector Bruce described it "as more noise than music."

After that inspection tour, Bruce begrudged teachers every cent they were paid. He stated in his report to the school board: "Three hundred dollars per year is money poorly spent."

LAUGHING

Most of us have embarrassed ourselves once or twice by taking a fit of laughter at an awkward and most inappropriate moment. But I doubt any of us faced such serious consequences for laughing as Captain John Skaling and his crew.

Captain John Hollis Skaling was from Nova Scotia's Kempt Shore, and in the 1860s he was regularly back and forth to the Caribbean and South America, sailing the long-established trading routes. He had met his wife in Brazil and so had a fancy for going back, bringing his wife with him.

On of one of his trips to Brazil, Captain Skaling and his crew attended a public ceremony. And right at the beginning, Captain Skaling took to laughing. He laughed at nothing in particular, but a bubble of mirth rose in his body, and laughter squeaked from his lips.

His laughter was infectious. Soon the entire crew bent double with laughter. The Brazilians thought captain and crew were laughing at the Brazilian flag. Without hesitation, they clapped Skaling and his crew in irons and tossed them into a disease-ridden South American jail. There was no trial, simply a life sentence to hell.

The British embassy rallied behind the sailors, and within a few weeks had them released. The British consul explained to Brazilian authorities that the laughter was unconnected with the raising of the the Brazilian national flag.

Captain Skaling later told the diplomat that had the crew not been released as soon as they had, they would surely have either died from disease or starved to death. He described one meal: a bull's head boiled and served on a platter with the horns and hide still attached. And that story got captain and crew laughing again—non-stop.

CAPE BRETON INGENUITY

Most often a bear will turn tail and run at the smell and sight of humans, so when one stands its ground, you can pretty well bet it has something to protect and will likely attack.

On November 12, 1812, James Pace and his brother Frederick went partridge hunting out around Huntington Mountain, Cape Breton. They had just cleared the trees and come onto a burned-over thicket of briers and scrub fir when a mighty bear rose on its hind legs, growled, and then attacked.

Frederick was the closest. With one swipe, the bear ripped off one of Frederick's coat sleeves and left his arm a mangled mass of bloody flesh. As Frederick fell to the ground, James got a clear shot. He raised his musket and fired—birdshot, about as good for killing a three-hundred-pound bear as raw eggs are for knocking holes in a barn door.

The bear now turned on James. James had all he could do to keep that bear a musket-length away from ripping him to pieces.

Meanwhile, Frederick drew himself to his knees, tore a brass button off his coat, and chewed it into the shape of a musket ball. He loaded and fired.

That chewed button struck the bear under the right eye and sent all three hundred pounds sprawling to the ground, writhing in agony. Then James came up from behind, gripped his musket against the bear's throat, and together the brothers strangled the bear out of its misery.

Afterward, and according to the *Acadian Recorder,* Frederick Pace wore that shredded coat wherever he went. When he told the story of the bear, he would hold out his torn coat sleeve and roll it up to show the scars on his right arm. Then he would smile, and point to the missing button from his coat as a way of drawing attention to his Cape Breton ingenuity.

AUTOMOBILES

In 1866, Father G. A. Belcourt, a Roman Catholic priest, turned the heads of his Rustico, Prince Edward Island, parishioners when he arrived at the St. Jean Baptiste picnic driving a steam-powered horseless carriage. He had bought the automobile in Philadelphia, and that purchase made Father Belcourt the first Canadian motorist.

For the next forty years, there was never more than one automobile on Prince Edward Island. Folks considered it a novelty, and some even paid ten cents to ride at county fairs. But in 1905, the Island became overrun with automobiles. There was a grand total of five gasoline-powered cars travelling Island roads. And as far as Islanders were concerned, that was four cars too many.

Islanders preferred the stink of horse manure to gasoline. And the chug, clang, and clatter seemed deafening compared to the gentle sound of horse hooves on the red Island roads.

People blamed every social problem imaginable on the automobile. Businessmen blamed a slump in the economy on farmers staying away from market for fear of encountering an automobile on the road and it spooking their horses. The Reverend Mr. Fullerton blamed the automobile for scaring his congregation into remaining home on Sunday mornings.

In 1908, Island legislators banned all automobiles from public streets and highways—all seven of them. And that law stayed on the books until 1913, when the New Automobile Act permitted automobiles on certain roads, but only three days a week—Monday, Wednesday, and Thursday. The law banned driving on Tuesdays and Fridays because they were market days, and on Saturday and Sunday because Saturday was for shopping and Sunday for church. The new law also left it up to individual communities whether to allow automobiles on their roads at all. Some communities did and some did not. That seemed to confuse the issue. It also put automobile drivers at a considerable disadvantage. For example, Fernwood Walter Heard had to hitch a horse to his car and haul it to the next settlement so he could take his new auto for a drive.

The enmity for automobiles bordered on the irrational. In 1918, one Bedeque woman attended a public meeting to oppose new legislation that would give automobiles the right to use public roads. She said: "We're going to keep them cars out if we have to take a pitchfork and drive it through them."

Even with this new legislation, people still shook their fists at a passing car and hollered from the roadside—"Get a horse!"

ZOOLOGICAL GARDEN

Andrew Downs was a Halifax plumber who cared more about nature and wildlife than about drain ditches and running water. From the time he was fourteen years old, Andrew had a dream—to build a magnificent zoological garden to display the exotic animals of the world.

In 1847, he acquired five acres on Dutch Village Road in Armdale, a subdivision of Halifax, Nova Scotia, and there he started his zoo, the first in North America. It soon became a resort for nature lovers. By 1863, Downs's zoological garden had grown to one hundred acres.

European royalty strolled the grounds, and stood aghast at the variety of animals: Skye terriers, Chinese and Egyptian geese and cranes, Brazilian monkeys. There were rare breeds of ducks and pheasants. There were beavers, minks, otters, black bears, moose, caribou, and elk, as well as Spanish, Mexican, and Virginian deer. Downs also built a waterfall to provide cool refreshment for a large polar bear.

The Halifax zoo became so famous that in 1867, the city of New York offered Andrew Downs the job of building a similar menagerie in Central Park.

Downs took the job. He sold all his property in Halifax, including his animals, and went to New York to lay the groundwork for the Central Park Zoo. But three months later he was back in Halifax, living at the corner of Inglis Street and Tower Road.

New York was fine, Andrew explained, as far as cities go, and the Central Park Zoo was interesting, but neither New York City nor its zoo stacked up well enough to the zoo he had built in Halifax.

KNOWING ONE'S CUSTOMERS

The business firm of Ellis and Chanter controlled day-to-day life at Biddeford, Prince Edward Island. Ellis ran the shipbuilding side of the business, which was the principal employer in the town, and Chanter managed the town's only store. Chanter sold everything from harnesses and ploughs to fancy dresses and hard candy. He bought livestock and grain from the farmers, and sold milk, butchered beef, flour, and other foodstuffs to the labourers in Ellis's shipyard. He also sold the farmers what they needed to keep farming. And as usual, the farmers bought more from Chanter than they sold to him.

In 1818, Chanter hired James Yeo to oversee the beef side of the business. Yeo was not much older than a boy, but he knew cattle. He travelled from farm to farm, buying livestock. He got along well with farmers and their families. The young man thought nothing of rolling up his sleeves and helping a farmer muck out a cattle barn or pitch a load of hay. Then, over tea, he would sit and talk, learning about the people he did business with, and appreciating their struggles to make ends meet.

A few years later, Chanter wanted out of the business so he could return to England. He owed James Yeo nine hundred pounds in back wages, and offered to trade his debt to Yeo in exchange for all the debts the farmers and labourers owed the store.

James Yeo required little time to think about it. He trusted the honesty and pride of the people he had come to know. He took the deal—and never looked back.

James Yeo collected every penny of those debts, and that gave him the start he needed to buy out Ellis's shipbuilding business.

Soon he was sending ships and supplies the world over. James Yeo became a very wealthy man because he took the time to know his customers.

OVERLAND SAIL

Captain John MacDonald lived at North Grant, about three miles from Antigonish, Nova Scotia. And in 1853, Captain John took a notion to build a sailing ship. North Grand is inland, and the captain lived on a farm, and that presented something of a problem when the time came for launching his farm-built schooner.

Captain MacDonald had laboured a few years at building that ship. He'd cut timber from his property and hand-hewed the beams and boards himself. When it came time to launch the thirty-ton schooner, Captain John spread the word around the countryside.

Hundreds showed up on launch day. Some came to gawk at the spectacle, but most came with willing hands. They raised the ship on a large platform, used thick logs as rollers, and with 160 head of oxen at the heave-ho, the captain and his hundred-man crew aimed the bow for the coast.

They sailed overland under full rigging, with flags flying and people cheering at every mile. The schooner slowly moved from North Grant through Antigonish, down Hawthorne Street to Main Street, until it reached the bridge on the east end of town. That was one obstacle Captain John had not figured on confronting, and it darn near scuttled his long-awaited launch. Then someone had a solution. In less than two hours, a couple dozen men reinforced the bridge.

The ship sailed on and on, at last reaching the coast. Before the largest crowd ever to attend a launch in Antigonish County, Captain John broke a bottle of bubbly against the hull. He christened the schooner *Sea Bird*, and for many years after, Captain John MacDonald's farm-built schooner served as a packet boat between Antigonish and Halifax.

STRANGE HANGING

In the early days in the Maritimes, the hanging of a criminal was relatively simple. The executioner slipped the noose over the condemned criminal's neck and hauled on the rope. A few inches off the ground was all that was necessary, but usually the hangman raised the condemned high in the air for spectators to get a good look at him kicking out his life. The strangling sometimes took up to an hour, unless the condemned had the good sense and the financial means to tip the hangman to pull down on the legs and speed up the process.

In later years, some provinces introduced the drop system, using the standard gallows and trap door affair. New Brunswick in 1827, however, had its own method for hanging a criminal; at least it did on one occasion.

In the summer of 1827, Patrick Burgan, an eighteen-year-old, slipped into a boarding house in Saint John and stole a pair of shoes. Not a serious crime by today's standards. Today, Pat Burgan would get a month in jail at most, or a stiff tongue-lashing from the judge at least. This was not the case in 1827, and certainly not with Judge Ward Chipman, who had a reputation for meting out stiff sentences.

For stealing one pair of shoes, Judge Chipman sentenced Patrick Burgan "...to hang by the neck until dead, dead, dead."

On the appointed morning, February 28, 1828, many spectators braved the cold and gathered outside the jailhouse. And according to the Saint John newspaper, half the crowd were women who had come to watch the hanging.

But there was not a whole lot to watch. No long, sad procession through the jail yard to the gallows. There was no gallows of any sort. Not even a tree. The executioner simply tied a rope to an iron ring inside the jailhouse and slipped the noose around Pat Burgan's neck. Then he threw the boy out the second-floor window. And that was that.

ISOLATION

The peace and tranquility of life on Prince Edward Island does have its downside—a complaint Islanders have voiced since the first days of settlement, and up until the building of the new bridge to the mainland. For some, the downside to Island life was isolation, especially during the long, hard winters.

Ferry crossings during good weather were common. But as soon as the temperature dropped and a thick floe of ice formed in the Northumberland Strait, Islanders felt closed off to the outside world. The Island became a community imprisoned behind an ice-crusted wall.

Such isolation was an obstacle for immigration to the Island. Progress demanded a growing population, and nothing swells a population like a flood of immigrants.

In February 1775, Governor Patterson ordered the crossing of the frozen Northumberland Strait by boat. He wanted to show Islanders and future immigrants that winter crossings were possible. He also wanted to open up a winter mail service. If nothing else, news from the outside world would punch a hole through the ice wall of isolation.

Seven men set out that winter, and made the crossing handily. But one crossing proved only that it could be done. A second crossing and a third would prove it could be regular.

Two years later, in February 1777, Acting Governor Phillip Callbeck persuaded a military officer named Stewart and two other men to attempt a winter crossing to Nova Scotia—in a small canoe, the way the Mi'kmaq had done it centuries before.

"A second success," Callbeck wrote, "will be a means of removing an objection which many people have made against living here."

Stewart and his crew crossed from Wood Islands to Pictou Island without a hitch, and that feat opened the door for regular winter crossings and a regular winter mail service.

The mail service was so important to relieving Islanders of winter isolation that the mail carrier played a valued role in Island life. His was a great responsibility, and to fulfill it dutifully came with high regard.

In March 1855, early one Friday morning, an iceboat left Cape Tormentine, New Brunswick, for Borden, Prince Edward Island, against a mild wind and light snow flurries. The iceboat had four crewmembers. It carried three passengers (Harry Hazard, Richard Johnston, and William Weir), as well as the Royal Mail.

By noon they were mid-strait, when the wind picked up. The snow flurries thickened, and pretty soon a wild blizzard was screaming down on them. Visibility was zero. The iceboat got turned around in the whiteout, and was within two miles of the ferry dock at Borden without the crew even realizing it.

Exhausted, they pulled the iceboat onto a raft of ice to wait out the storm. And there they floated while the blizzard raged and the temperature dropped.

For three days they floated, frozen to the bone and starved. On Sunday, they killed Weir's dog for the blood and raw flesh.

And still they floated. Harry Hazard became delirious from the hunger and cold. By Monday night, he was dead.

Later that night, their boat pulled up in Fox Harbour, Nova Scotia, hardly twenty-five miles from where they had first set off. Two of the crew went for help. They trudged through deep snow, and came upon a farmhouse early that Tuesday morning.

The rescue party found Harry Hazard's frozen body upright in the snow. It marked the overturned iceboat, under which the others had huddled for warmth.

Throughout the entire ordeal, Bill McRae, one of the crew, had held fast to the Royal Mail pouch. Even after the rescue, he refused to let it go.

HARTLAND BRIDGE

(BJG)

Hartland, New Brunswick, boasts the longest covered bridge in the world. But it wasn't always a covered bridge, and it came close to never becoming one again.

In April 1920, a heavy ice jam on the St. John River swept away two spans of the long wooden bridge at Hartland. The government decided not just to repair it, but also to do things right and give it a roof and walls, thus adding many years to its life.

But the covering would make it into a kind of long, dark tunnel—and that's what brought down the wrath of this deeply religious community. William Carr, an engineer who helped build the bridge, wrote about the religious leaders: "...they thought it would provide a dark place where boys and girls might do things they were not supposed to do until married."

One local preacher was more colourful: he said the covering would turn the bridge into "a potential ram-pasture."

Extremists saw it as a den of Satan himself—the world's longest covered brothel. A petition asked the government to change its plans, and said: "...to cover the bridge would seriously jeopardize the morals of the young people of Hartland."

But government ignored the outcry.

A member of the New Brunswick legislature wrote to the New Brunswick Contracting and Building Company of Saint John, ordering the work to go as planned. He added: "If the morals of the young people are so badly bent that it only requires a covered bridge to break them then there is little the Government can do about the matter."

It has been nearly a century, and both Hartland's covered bridge and its morals have held up pretty well.

Marvels and Mysteries

FATE

Some say the when, where, and how of one's death is written down at the moment of one's birth; and that no matter how desperate the circumstances, if you're not fated to die, you won't.

In mid-November 1840, at Canso, Nova Scotia, that old saying proved true. It had to do with a fishing skiff finding a woman and a child huddled on the beach of Andrew Island. The woman was in shock and the child bawled for food. The fishermen took them to Canso. After a few days of food and tender care, the woman finally heaved a deep sigh and told her story.

Her name was Mrs. Walsh, and she had sailed with her husband and child from St. Peter's, Newfoundland, aboard the schooner *Spring Bird*. They were bound for Gabarus, Cape Breton. Her husband's family had a farm there. There were thirty other passengers aboard, and six crew.

In the telling of her story, Mrs. Walsh had several moments of confusion. She told of a storm. Heavy winds. A high sea. She said she heard a loud crash, and the squeal and splinter of wood. She grabbed her child, and at that moment the sea rushed over her.

She woke on the beach on Andrew Island with the child still in her arms.

A few days later, Canso fishermen found debris from the wrecked schooner—a plank and some broken timber. All aboard had perished except for the mother and child. The fishermen wondered how these two had managed to survive that raging sea. They spoke about it often, particularly when a storm blew up on the water.

Canso villagers did the same. For years after, whenever the subject of survival at sea arose in conversation, someone was sure to tell of Mrs. Walsh and her child, and several among them would smile and take comfort in knowing that no matter how desperate the circumstances threatening one's life, if it is not your time to go, you won't.

If you could ask Albert Boudreau if that was true, he would probably wrap his arms around himself as if in a hug, look off as though looking into the past, and nod his agreement. Albert Boudreau also survived a raging sea, and he always wondered how.

On a chilly morning in September 1933, a Judique, Nova Scotia, householder answered a knock at his front door. Sleep crusted his eyelids and his brain still moved in slow motion. As he swung open the door, his senses suddenly sharpened at the sight of a drenched and exhausted sailor who looked more dead than alive. The sailor was Albert Boudreau, second engineer aboard the *Hurry On*, a Halifax ship bound for Montreal with a cargo of corn.

"Four men," Boudreau said. "Four men on the beach." Then he passed out with exhaustion.

Boudreau and his four companions were the only survivors of a harrowing night at sea. The *Hurry On* had left Halifax the day before. Off the Cape Breton coast, it ran into gale-force winds and a heavy sea. The vessel tossed helplessly in the shallow, dangerous waters. Then the twelve-member crew abandoned ship for a lifeboat, and watched until the *Hurry On* went to the bottom.

The crew huddled in an open boat while the storm roared and the sea fumed. Twice the lifeboat swamped, and twice the men played out their strength to right it again and climb inside. Provisions and oars were swept overboard, and some men were lost in the dark and foaming waters. Others died from the battering and exhaustion.

"The first thing we would know," Albert Boudreau said, "a man would let go and disappear. And we were in no shape to hold him in the boat."

When the lifeboat scraped the beach at Judique, only five survived—five out of twelve in an open boat against a cruel sea. Until the day he finally gave up the ghost, Albert wondered why he was one of them.

MYSTERY LADY

Most people believed she was a wealthy European aristocrat scorned and abandoned by her family. Halifax knew her only by the name of Miss Floyer, though most suspected that that was not her real name.

She arrived in Halifax in 1780, accompanied by a young man who called himself Lieutenant Floyer. He was not part of any regiment stationed in Halifax. Lieutenant Floyer said very little about himself and nothing about Miss Floyer, an attractive woman in her mid-30s with raven hair and downcast eyes.

They immediately made their residence in a cottage on the old Preston Road outside the town, and lived completely in seclusion.

A year passed. Then one morning, Lieutenant Floyer walked to the waterfront, took passage on a ship bound for Jamaica, and never returned.

The woman continued in the same house, living in the same secluded way. Grocers delivered food and left it outside the door; the rent had been paid years in advance.

Then in October 1794, during the Napoleonic War, a British warship captured the French governor of the island of St. Pierre and brought him to Halifax. Because he was of noble birth, the Frenchman could live freely in the town, on the promise he would not try to escape. Of all the homes in Halifax where he could choose to live, he picked the cottage on the old Preston Road occupied by the mysterious lady.

The French governor lived there for more than fifteen years, and returned to France after Napoleon's defeat. He had taken part in much of Halifax's social life, but never said a word about the lady with whom he had shared accommodation.

Miss Floyer died in December 1814—her real name and story have ever remained a mystery.

TALL STORY

John Geddes often told the story of how, in 1827, he went hunting near Musquodoboit with his neighbour and friend Peter Coop. As Geddes tells the story, Peter Coop, a Mi'kmaq man, was a fine hunter, and once had guided British royalty on a hunting expedition in the Nova Scotia backcountry.

On this October day, Geddes and Coop made camp at Dollar Lake. Come morning, John Geddes awoke to find that Peter Coop had already gone off hunting on his own, and that he had left a marker on a tree to show Geddes the direction he had taken.

Just then Geddes heard a musket blast, and something told him there was trouble. He grabbed his musket and went off running. Sure enough, there was trouble.

Peter Coop had shot at a bear and only wounded it. He had tracked the bear into thick underbrush, where it was awkward for a hunter to level and aim his musket. He could hear the bear snarling, and was backing out of that thicket when the bear charged. It clawed and tore flesh off Peter Coop's backside as he ran. Then it grabbed the hunter in its fatal hug and squeezed.

Geddes arrived just then, but the thick brush kept him from getting a clear shot. He heard the snap of Coop's ribs, then saw Coop reach into the bear's mouth, grab its tongue, and hold on until that bear strangled to death. Peter Coop collapsed to the ground along with the bear. Coop was still alive, and lived for many years after.

"Unbelievable," was what most folks said, until John Geddes put his hand on a King James Bible, swore every word was true, then held up Peter Coop's breeches with the arse clawed out.

THE *CITY OF BOSTON*

On January 28, 1870, the *City of Boston,* an ocean liner, sailed out of Halifax bound for England. Now, ships follow certain sea lanes across the ocean, and it is quite common for ocean liners and freighters to pass within sight of each other. No ship saw the *City of Boston* during its crossing. There was no news about the *City of Boston* until late March, when there occurred a series of strange communications.

A telegraph reached Halifax announcing the ship's arrival at Queensland, Ireland. This was a curious telegraph indeed, because there was no record of it having ever been sent. And subsequent telegraphs from Ireland reported that the *City of Boston* had not arrived at any port in the British Isles.

A week later, another telegraph was sent from Queensland, Ireland, to Mrs. J. D. Purdy of King Street in Saint John, New Brunswick. It too told of the safe arrival of the *City of Boston* at Queensland.

Strange indeed, for the *City of Boston,* after departing Halifax, was never seen or heard from again—except for another strange communication a year later.

Mrs. Helen Harper Steeves of Shediac, New Brunswick, found a bottle on the beach with this message written on yellow copy paper:

"21st March. *City of Boston* sinking. Over half full of water now. Goodbye all. Look after my boy, Thompson. Be gone in two hours."

RELIGIOUS ENTHUSIASM

(BJG)

Sheffield is a farming settlement along the St. John River in central New Brunswick. In 1829, the settlement was going through a deep religious depression. Some said Sheffield had gone the way of the devil and that it would take something next to a miracle to turn Sheffield around.

In July of that year, a young farmer, Thomas B. Coburn, was cutting hay when a remarkably heavy thunderstorm suddenly hit. Coburn sought shelter under a huge elm at the end of his field.

A bolt of lightening struck the tree, followed down its trunk, leaped to Coburn's head, and then ran down his body. His boots exploded, and poor Coburn never knew what hit him.

A coroner's jury brought in the verdict that Thomas B. Coburn died "...by the visitation of Divine Providence."

Coburn was a general favourite in the community, which lamented his death. But it was that verdict, "death by Divine Providence" that made a deep impression. To all of Coburn's acquaintances, it brought home the awful power (and the immediacy) of that Divine Providence.

On the following Sunday, two local men and one woman ventured to attend the church they had ignored for several years—if not quite forgotten.

Their example made others braver, and within two weeks, twelve more attended, and, as the newspaper account says, "found peace with Divine Providence."

That was only the beginning. Religious enthusiasm mounted.

On the evening of August 27, 1829, at least three hundred people came to the Sunday service. The bolt that blew the boots off young Thomas B. Coburn prompted what the paper describes as "a sober sense of the Divine presence among the whole of the Sheffield community."

GHOST AT BLUE ROCKS

In 1910, the Reverend Canon Voorhees Evans Harris had completed the Sunday evening service at St. Barnabas Church in Blue Rocks, Lunenburg County, Nova Scotia. He was new to the parish, and stayed late to make a good impression on his parishioners. He had planned to return to Lunenburg on Monday morning, but Sunday evening was such a beautiful moonlit night that Canon Harris set off walking the five miles to Lunenburg at once.

After travelling three miles, he reached a section of road that ran straight for about half a mile. Up ahead, he saw a man driving a wagon. The man was alone and walking his horse at a slow pace. Canon Harris ran forward, expecting to hitch a ride to Lunenburg. In a letter to his bishop, he describes what happened next:

> I got to within a few yards and was just going to ask the man to give me a lift when the whole thing—man, wagon, and horse disappeared. It seemed to sink into the ground, and in another moment I was standing upon the spot where it had vanished.
>
> Next morning at the breakfast table, I mentioned the occurrence to a gentleman who managed a foundry in Lunenburg. He smiled at my story then said that several of his workers lived out that way and were in the habit of seeing the same phantom.
>
> Mrs. DeBlois, a native of Lunenburg, later told me that although she had never seen it herself, she knew lots of people who had.

According to legend, Canon Harris's apparition is the ghost of a peddler who met an accidental death on the road from Blue Rocks. It is said that he still travels that road in a horse and wagon rattling with pots and pans.

Legend or not, one wonders what the bishop thought when he read that letter from his young canon serving on the South Shore. A little too much sacramental wine, perhaps?

WRECK OF THE *HUNGARIAN*

Clark's Harbour is a small fishing village on Cape Sable Island along Nova Scotia's South Shore. Here, the coastline is about as ragged as ripped cloth, with dangerous reefs, shoals, submerged rocks, and tiny islands. The tides are unpredictable, and the winds and currents baffling.

On the night of February 1, 1858, a passenger ship, the *Hungarian*, steaming from Liverpool, England, to New York, ran on the Cape Sable reefs in a driving snowstorm. The hull split open like a sardine can, and filled within seconds. Then the ship rolled on its side in helpless submission to the raging sea.

Four hundred passengers howled for their lives against the wild wind, the pounding sea, and the squeal of twisting metal.

On shore, Cape Sable Islanders heard the screams of the passengers and the agony of the battered ship. Several times the fishermen tried launching their small boats and skiffs for a rescue, but each time the high sea and blowing snow drove them back to shore.

Late the following day, the storm quieted and the sea calmed. The ship was a mass of twisted ironwork submerged between two reefs. Of the four hundred passengers, only a few bodies had washed ashore.

It was several months before a wrecking steamer tried to recover some of the cargo. It brought up a single lump of dry goods weighing about seven tons. As the load cleared the water, a worker noticed a human foot dangling from the bottom. They cut away the mass and found inside the perfectly preserved body of a beautiful young woman. They buried her at Clark's Harbour in a nameless grave, another victim to the treacherous waters of Nova Scotia's coast.

CANADA'S FIRST BANK ROBBERY

On the morning of August 11, 1849, two men on their way to work on the Halifax waterfront crossed the intersection at Storey's Corner on Water Street, about one block north of Duke Street, and found two bags of money. Stamped on the canvas bags was "The Halifax Banking Company." As it turned out, the bank did not even know the money was missing.

The Halifax Banking Company was Canada's first bank. And this was Canada's first bank robbery.

According to Detective Jack Power, the thief must have been a professional, because he had picked the locks on nine doors in the bank, including the vault. Then the thief relocked every door on his way out. Detective Power figured the money found at Storey's Corner must have been two bags more than the thief could carry.

Detective Power investigated for more than a month without discovering a single clue.

Then, about twelve years later, a fellow from Australia stopped Detective Power near the Egg Pond on the Halifax Common and told Power he had been a prison guard in Australia. He said an ex-convict had once bragged that his greatest haul of money was from a bank in Halifax, Nova Scotia. Unfortunately, the Australian prison guard did not remember the ex-con's name.

And that's about as close as Detective Power or anyone else ever came to knowing who pulled Canada's first bank job.

THE STRANGE DEATH OF MARVIN THOMAS

(BJG)

Tracy Station is on the rail line linking Saint John and Montreal. There, on the night of May 12, 1917, the home of Marvin Thomas burned to the ground. The next day, searchers found his charred remains in the ashes.

At a brief coroner's inquest, Mrs. Thomas said her husband Marvin kept Paris Green, a powerful bug killer heavy on arsenic, and that he somehow had managed to poison himself and burn down the house.

Nasty rumours circulated, and the coroner, John Murphy, ordered another inquest. This time, Mrs. Thomas said her late husband had threatened to kill the whole family, including himself, and that, being afraid, she rescued the things she valued—the children, the cattle, a horse, and a gramophone. It was also revealed that Mrs. Thomas, who was middle-aged, had a boyfriend. He was Frank Money, aged twenty-one, and on the night of the fire, she and young Money were out driving until 2:00 AM. She and Money were charged with murder.

At the preliminary hearing, Mrs. Thomas's daughter, sixteen-year-old Violet, said there had been an argument before the fire, and that her father had hit her mother on the head with a rifle.

But there was still no clear evidence of murder.

Then the provincial pathologist revealed that he had made a mistake during the coroner's inquest. He said he had examined the dead man's lungs and found no poison, but later when he examined the stomach (which he had earlier mistaken for the heart), he found carbolic acid in it.

The magistrate simply shook his head at the man's incompetence and decided the death was just what Mrs. Thomas had said it was—a suicide. Case dismissed.

The following month, Mrs. Thomas and Frank Money got married.

MIRAMICHI GHOST

(BJG)

In the winter of 1857, a man named Duncan joined a lumber crew along the Miramichi River in New Brunswick. As a day's work drew to its end, a sudden snow squall (a big one) struck, and the crew headed for camp. All but Duncan; he remembered he had left his axe against a brow in the bog some fifty yards back, and went to get it.

The squall thickened, darkness fell fast, and soon Duncan realized he had wandered off the road. As he groped in the snow-blind darkness, there came to him on the wind what sounded like a voice, one calling from far away. He listened. It was a voice—a voice like that of a man teaming a pair of horses.

Duncan ran toward the voice. Then suddenly, out of the snow and darkness, he made out a huge, dark shape close beside him—a team of horses. They were hooked to a huge log, and atop the log stood the driver. Duncan spoke, but got no answer.

He followed the team and driver for a quarter mile, and hit the woods road that led back to camp. Then, to Duncan's amazement, the driver's voice quieted and the team disappeared.

In camp that night, Duncan drew up near the open fire and told his story about the axe, the storm, and the ghostly team and driver that had guided him back to the lumber road. A semicircle of fire-lit faces focused on Duncan. They listened intently and in sober silence. Heads nodded in perfect understanding. These men had spent their working lifetimes in the dark forests of the Miramichi. They knew things like that could happen here.

A MERCHANT SAILOR

Most men and women who served in the Canadian navy during World War Two will say straight out that the merchant sailors who manned those poorly armed freighters between North America and the war effort in Europe were the bravest of the brave. These freighters carried troops, supplies, and armaments to Europe, and sailed in convoys for protection. They were the principle targets of the German U-boats that preyed the North Atlantic in "wolf packs."

The merchant sailors knew the danger and bravely accepted their fate, but none as much as an unknown sailor aboard the steamer *Donald Stewart*.

In 1942, the *Donald Stewart*, sailing in convoy, cruised into the Strait of Belle Isle, bound for Goose Bay, Labrador. It carried a cargo of airplanes and high-test gasoline. The convoy was about midway through the strait when the escort ship, the corvette *Weyburn*, spotted a U-boat (U-517) lying in shallow water.

Before the corvette could turn and attack, the U-boat fired two torpedoes. The *Donald Stewart* took the hit in the stern and bow. The explosion was frightening, but what followed next was even more so. As a boatload of survivors pulled away from the torpedoed ship, the gasoline ignited and exploded. Flames now engulfed the ship and surrounding water. Fire roared.

Suddenly, a door opened in the afterhouse of the burning ship. A man stepped out. He wore a topcoat and top hat, and carried a suitcase. According to those on board the *Weyburn,* the man looked around at the burning ship and over the side at the flames on the water. Then, without showing alarm or despair, he waved to his mates in the lifeboat, and re-entered the cabin as the burning *Donald Stewart* sank into the cold North Atlantic.

SWEARIN' SAM

(BJG)

In New Brunswick's early lumber woods, few men would work with a man who swore. Too many times they'd heard a man utter a frightful curse then, moments later, watched him die a frightful death.

These roughnecks might not have loved the Lord—but they certainly feared him.

One of the "cursingest" men ever in those lumber woods was named Sam Masters. He worked on the Miramichi in the 1850s, and he was tolerated because "Swearin' Sam," as they called him, was among the best teamsters the men had ever seen.

As darkness set in one winter's afternoon in 1857, there was only one huge log left to be dragged to the brow, and the crew decided to leave it till morning—all but Swearin' Sam. He swore he'd take that log out alone "or have breakfast in hell."

Back at camp, the men weren't really surprised that Sam didn't show up for supper. They waited until about eight o'clock, and then a small party set out under the bright moon to hunt for Sam.

They hadn't far to go. There in the hauling road stood the team, still hitched to the big log. Then someone spotted a pair of larrigans sticking out from under one side of the log and Sam's head and crushed chest from the other. It was a horrible sight.

The next morning, they wrapped the corpse in a blanket and hauled it out to the settlement. As they buried Swearin' Sam, each man remembered that Sam's last words were a curse—something about hauling that goddamn log by nightfall or having breakfast in hell. And the sight of Sam being lowered into the grave reinforced their fear of the Lord.

MACDOUGALL'S VISION

Donnie MacDougall was from Broad Cove, Inverness County, Nova Scotia, and he had the gift of second sight—he could see things that would happen in the future. Most of his friends and neighbours firmly believed this, because more than a dozen times over the past ten or fifteen years, Donnie's visions had come true.

Sometime in the 1890s, Donnie overlooked the coast at Broad Cove and had a vision. It was different from his other visions in that this one was not as clear and distinct. One thing was certain, however: Donnie saw a long, black object sinking through the ice at Broad Cove.

"A boat," his friends and neighbours surmised. "A black boat!"

Now, there were no black boats along that coast, so most in Inverness County felt pretty safe from Donnie's vision.

Then about two weeks later, Archie Gillis bought a dark-blue boat and rigged it for fishing. Most folks figured this was the boat from Donnie MacDougall's vision. Dark blue, they said, was close enough to black.

So the morning Archie set sail, a crowd gathered to see him off, behaving as though they were seeing him for the last time. But nothing happened. And for many years thereafter, Archie safely fished with that dark-blue boat, and then sold it and bought a red one.

It was another twenty years before the truth of Donnie MacDougall's vision became known. That winter, a long, black object slid off the road at Broad Cove, plunged through the ice, and sank in the exact spot of Donnie MacDougall's vision. It was a car—one of the first on Cape Breton Island.

WANG RASMUSSEN

Wang Rasmussen was a Danish-born Canadian who lived in Fox Harbour, Nova Scotia. He had moved there in 1926. During World War Two, he served in the Royal Canadian Navy, and when the war was over, he went back to farming in Fox Harbour, and to carpentry.

Wang was a fair hand with a saw and chisel. He could build anything: houses, furniture, even boats.

For Wang, the war had been a great adventure against which common, ordinary, everyday life did not quite measure up.

In 1949, he started building a boat—a thirty-foot sloop—and he meant to sail the Atlantic Ocean single-handed. He wanted to sail to Denmark on an adventure, the way his Viking ancestors had done.

Friends and neighbours tried to talk him out of it, but Wang Rasmussen was stubborn. He set the date for sailing—October 18, 1951—and stuck to it. Despite the bad weather brewing outside the harbour, and with his deck loaded with potatoes (Wang thought potatoes would make a good cash crop in Denmark), he sailed out of Fox Harbour and was never heard from or seen again.

He had promised to cable from St. John's, Newfoundland, but he never even made it that far.

Rumour always seems to follow mishap, and the rumours were not far behind Wang's disappearance. Some said Wang Rasmussen was a Russian spy who had been picked up by a Russian sub once he cleared the Nova Scotia coast. But that was just wild talk at a time when everyone was afraid of Russians.

No, Wang Rasmussen was just a common, ordinary man who, in his later years, wanted for a little adventure in his life.

Don't we all.

UNKNOWN WOMAN

The provincial penitentiary on the Northwest Arm (an ocean inlet that makes Halifax, Nova Scotia, a peninsula) has long since disappeared. Not many even know it ever existed. Authorities closed its doors in 1867, and most of its cut-granite blocks went into other buildings throughout the city.

From the 1840s to 1860s, this penitentiary imprisoned some of the most ruthless cutthroats in Nova Scotia history. It also held a mysterious young woman who strangely held the respect and admiration of guards, prison officials, and inmates alike. Who she was and what crime she had committed has been lost in the rubbing dust of history. Yet her memory lived on long after her death in the 1850s.

She was buried outside the prison walls near the shore of the Northwest Arm. A black iron railing surrounded her grave, and prison authorities and former inmates maintained and decorated it with flowers for more than thirty years after the prison was closed.

By the twentieth century, her grave had become a barren, windswept patch of ground, unnoticed by those who passed by.

Who was she, and what had she done that her memory lived for so long in the hearts of prison officials and hardened criminals? Unfortunately, the prison records provide not a single clue. And so the unmarked grave of the unknown woman on the shore of Halifax's Northwest Arm remains a mystery.

THE VERDICT

(BJG)

Thomas Wooden and his wife lived in a small house at Hoyt, a rural community in southern Sunbury County, New Brunswick. The couple had been married many years, and for most of those years did not get along well together.

After her husband's sudden death, Mrs. Wooden told the coroner's jury of events on that fatal day. The couple slept in different rooms, and the wife said that, as usual, she arose first, went to the kitchen, made porridge, then called her husband to breakfast.

On this particular day, however, no reply came from the husband's room. Climbing the stairs, she found Thomas still in bed. His hand held a revolver resting on his chest. There was a bullet hole in the side of his head, and he was very much dead.

Despite the smallness of the house, Mrs. Wooden heard no gunshot, or so she told the inquest.

The coroner's jury heard the evidence, including that of the local physician, Dr. Dundas. The jury deliberated and came to the conclusion that the victim came to his death by suicide. Thomas Wooden was buried in the local cemetery.

But nasty rumours circulated in the small community. They were so persistent that the sheriff decided further investigation was in order. He ordered the coroner, H. H. Pride, to call a second inquest. The body was exhumed.

This time the coroner called in two physicians. After careful examination, they discovered not just one, but two bullet holes in the side of Thomas Wooden's head.

Again the coroner's jury retired and solemnly deliberated, and again they brought in the same verdict: "The victim came to his death by suicide."

And once again, the little village buried Thomas Wooden.

EBENEZER HATHEWAY

Ebenezer Hatheway was a Loyalist officer during the American Revolution. During the Battle of Harlem Heights in New York, he and eight British soldiers rowed a small boat on a scout up the East River. They ran smack into six or seven American whaleboats loaded with retreating Continental soldiers. Hatheway and his crew fought it out until they were simply overpowered.

As was the practice then, the Patriots took the British soldiers as prisoners, and either paroled them on their oath not to take up arms against the Patriot cause again or exchanged them for some of their own who had been captured by the other side. Ebenezer Hatheway, however, was a different catch altogether. Hatheway was a Loyalist, a fellow American who had volunteered to fight against his neighbours. To American eyes, he was a traitor pure and simple, and deserved the worst punishment they could give him.

And that's just what he got. The Patriots bound him, leashed him, and led him across backcountry Connecticut to a place fifteen miles outside Hartford. It was a dungeon in every respect, the most dreaded prison in the colonies—Simsbury Mine.

On first sight, it seemed harmless enough: a guardhouse of squared timber with fifteen to twenty jailers inside who kept a close eye on the trap door in the centre. The trap led down to a small room with more guards and another trap door. This trap had iron ringbolts and thick iron bars threaded through. It took two men to raise it with a block and tackle. The hinges grated and groaned under the weight of so much iron.

As Ebenezer stood at this threshold, all of a sudden Simsbury Mine turned horribly grim. He buckled at the stink rising on the torchlight, a foul blast of what was to come.

Six feet below, down a ladder greasy with dampness and mud, he stood at a large iron grate over a three-foot-wide shaft through solid rock. Here the stink was worse—human filth and rot.

The second hatch opened, and the guards pushed and prodded him down the next ladder, which dropped thirty-eight feet to a landing and a tunnel that descended another thirty feet to what the prisoners called "the woeful mansion." This was a dark cavern in iron-grey rock, a hopeless pit down a seventy-four-foot shaft in the earth. This was hell, a living hell, and like hell there was no getting out—except, here, by being dragged up the ladders as a corpse.

For more than a year, Ebenezer Hatheway lived with shadows and voices and the painful drip of groundwater counting out the moments. He ate what he could scoop from a bucket and hold in both hands. He slept on straw spread over smooth stone, and warmed himself by a pot of charcoal. For the first year, he hungered for news from above and fed off the rumours the guards threw down the shaft like bones. But for the next year, he lived simply to survive. The future had become little more than a dim lozenge of daylight down an auger hole bored from the surface. The world above had become a memory fading like the echo of footfalls along the tunnel.

Then one day, in a halo of torchlight, an angel appeared, a nameless woman dressed in grey muslin and a dark-green shawl. She was sister to an unspeaking prisoner in that hellhole, and she had bargained with the guards for the benefit of visiting her kin.

Late each day, the guards allowed her to descend the ladders through the trap doors to the pit below, where her brother lay hacking out his lungs against the iron-grey rock. With each visit, she left behind a wooden club that she had hemmed into the folds of her skirt, and once she delivered the prisoners a knife. She had a plan as well.

One dark evening (at the time ordered for her departure), Ebenezer and his fellows crept quietly along the tunnel and climbed the ladder behind her. They were armed with sharp stones, the wooden clubs the woman had brought, and the knife.

At her call, the guard opened the first trap door, and before he could holler a warning, Ebenezer pulled him through the hatch and to his death thirty-eight feet below. The woman called again at the second trap door, and the prisoners quietly waited for the guards to throw the bars through the ringbolts and haul the trap open with the tackle. They burst into the room with stones flying and clubs flailing. They were desperate men who overpowered the two jailers and charged up the next ladder to the guardhouse above. They charged against fifteen men and fifteen muskets. Charged because they had nothing left to lose. Charged against death with their eyes wide open, moving faster than the guards, swinging quicker, threatening louder. Six prisoners fell to a musket blast. But there was no retreat, no going back down that ladder to hell. So they charged again, stunning the guards—just for a moment, just long enough to wrestle the muskets away.

They were twenty-three men, and a woman whose name Ebenezer had failed to ask, what with the fever of the fight in the guardhouse still running in his blood and all the worry of being one hundred miles behind enemy lines. The escaped prisoners and the woman separated into three groups to increase the chance that some would escape to the safety of New York.

For seventeen days, Ebenezer and five others clawed through the thickest of the Connecticut backcountry. They kept off the beaten path until they hit a British outpost at Yonkers. Ebenezer was on Long Island a few days later, and there he remained for the last few years of the Revolutionary War.

On most of those New York nights, Ebenezer Hatheway thanked his lucky stars for the individual bravery of that woman. He swore to God that after the war, after British might ground this rebellion to slag, he would scout every Connecticut village and farm for that woman and thank her for giving him his life.

But the war dragged on and on. British victory gave way to stalemate, and stalemate to defeat. Ebenezer's promise cracked with the bad news from Yorktown about Cornwallis's surrender. And it broke with the rebels shrieking, scolding, and mocking him and thousands of other Loyalists into exile in New Brunswick.

Here, Ebenezer Hatheway made a new start with a new family, stacking hope against the loss and sorrow of the past. Here he lifted his heavy feet across the newly ploughed fields of his land grant at Burton in Sunbury County. Here he danced clumsily before an October fire, with the harvest in the barn, and a wife all arms and lifting her face for love.

As Justice of the Peace and captain of the local militia, Ebenezer had ample opportunity to meet and talk with new settlers to Sunbury and York counties, and just about anyone else passing through. Ebenezer would often start off a conversation with someone new by asking if the person had ever heard tell of a woman who helped twenty-three men escape the Simsbury Mine.

In 1811, Ebenezer Hatheway died not knowing who that woman was. Though he was old and sick and bone-tired of living his last ten years with pain, some say his last words were to bless the memory of the brave woman who had saved him from the Simsbury Mine.

Rogues and Rascals

THE *FAIRY QUEEN*

The *Fairy Queen* was a side-wheeler, a steamboat with paddlewheels on both sides, that sailed between Charlottetown, Prince Edward Island, and Pictou, Nova Scotia. On October 8, 1853, it departed Charlottetown with the inauspicious number of thirteen passengers and thirteen crew.

The day was dark, and a high wind increased in force as the *Fairy Queen* crossed the Northumberland Strait. Except for the rolling sea, all seemed well, the passengers making light on the main deck. Still the winds rose, now blowing a squall that had the crew bailing the engine room. Then at Gull Rock, near Pictou Island, a strong gust broke the tiller rope, disengaging the steering mechanism. The *Fairy Queen* broached broadside to the wind, and the engine room flooded.

The engines stopped, and the *Fairy Queen* bobbed helpless on the churning sea.

The passengers helped with the bailing, but even that was nothing against the flood of water over the sides. Fear took hold, then panic. The officers and crew suddenly ran for the lifeboats, lowering them and clambering over the sides to save their own lives.

Mr. Lidiard, a passenger, cried for the crew to pull alongside to take the ladies. The crew's response was to lower their oars and pull the lifeboats further away from the powerless steamer.

For more than an hour, waves pounded and pounded on the drifting hull. The stranded passengers screamed, prayed, and wished their goodbyes to one another and to their distant families. Then the *Fairy Queen* cracked in two and sank.

Of the thirteen passengers, only Lidiard and four others managed to cling to the wreckage that remained afloat until the storm subsided. They washed ashore at Merigomish Island.

Weeks later, Lidiard and the surviving passengers paraded into court in Charlottetown, where they told about the sinking, and how the captain and crew had willingly abandoned them to the wreck of the *Fairy Queen*.

JUST GOOD LUCK

Two centuries ago there was no fingerprinting, no matching of blood samples, no DNA testing. Back then, police work was mostly a matter of eyewitness accounts and good luck.

In the spring of 1815, Bill Sabatier was high sheriff of Halifax County, and investigating a foul and brutal murder on the Cobequid Road. His investigation amounted to asking neighbours if anyone had seen a stranger, and if they had, which way did he go.

As luck would have it, someone told Sabatier about a stranger in the Cobequid Tavern. The sheriff slipped into the tavern unnoticed and collared the stranger, a man named Wilson, and charged him with murder.

Wilson vehemently denied it. That was expected—but what he said next wasn't. He said he was not going to hang for a crime he did not commit. He then admitted to being a professional thief, but insisted he was not a murderer.

Sheriff Sabatier drew up a chair and listened as Wilson explained how he operated.

Wilson said he followed the cattle drovers to the Halifax market. These were the men contracted to supply beef to the military. They usually returned to their farms in the Shubenacadie Valley with a saddlebag stuffed with money. Wilson either robbed them along the roadside or as they slept in roadhouses and inns.

He confessed to recently robbing a cattleman at McAlpine's Road House at the junction of Lady Hammond Road and the Windsor Highway. He also confessed to half a dozen other robberies over the past two years.

"Robbery, yes," Wilson cried, "but not murder!"

Sheriff Sabatier shrugged. Robbery, murder, they're both the same to the hangman. He charged Wilson with murder and six counts of robbery. In one fell swoop, Sabatier had solved more than half a dozen crimes with good old-fashioned luck.

SMUGGLING

A rough and jagged coastline seems divinely made for smugglers. And there is no coastline more jagged than Nova Scotia's. From the first days of settlement, smuggling was a problem for honest merchants who could not compete against it, and for the government that could not stamp it out.

In 1768, the Nova Scotia Executive Council wrote the Colonial Office in London, explaining why smuggling was so prevalent: "... if one cargo was got clear and another was taken, the owners were gainers, at least they were no losers. And if they got two barrels clear for one being caught they gained much more than they could do by entering it legally."

On March 6, 1797, a handful of representatives from Annapolis County gathered at Fred Sinclair's tavern in Annapolis Royal. Fred served rum and listened to their complaints against smugglers, and even helped draft the petition they would later send to the government in Halifax.

One merchant complained that he could not remember when a trading vessel was not involved in smuggling. Another man marked down the time the sloop *Betsy* opened a tavern on deck and openly sold cordials from barrels of smuggled rum.

Fred Sinclair added his voice. He recalled the Philadelphia smuggler who arrived each year in a ship of seventy tons, a sizable ship for a smuggler, and set up shop for three weeks selling contraband goods unmolested.

Then Fred explained how rum merchants and tavern keepers stocked barrels of rum that had cleared customs years before. The barrels had been stamped with the King's Broad Arrow as proof of their clearance. The merchants would simply refill these barrels with smuggled booze.

All heads nodded agreement as someone added a few more complaints to the petition. Then Fred served a round of drinks as all signed their names, sealed the document, and sent it on the next packet boat to Halifax. Fred poured off another round so they could toast their effort. This was from his private stock. The best of Jamaica rum, and every barrel of it had been smuggled.

HALIFAX'S BRAVEST MEN

When it comes to bravery, the Americans might have their Daniel Boone and Davy Crockett, but Nova Scotia has Reuben Hemsley and Thomas Wiseman—two of the bravest men to ever set foot in the province, and two of the most eager to suck down a jug of rum.

In October 1751, Hemsley and Wiseman were sitting in their four-by-four shack on Halifax's waterfront and listening to the musket fire and war whoops coming from the Dartmouth side. Just then, a couple of buildings went up in flames. In the orange glow over the water, the two men could see rowboats loaded with Dartmouth settlers pulling for the Halifax shore.

Now, Hemsley and Wiseman were suffering a powerful thirst. They had already gone a full day after draining their last jug of rum. And the musket fire and war whoops and the sight of the Dartmouth settlers on the water had both men thinking the same thought—John Coleman's Tavern.

Coleman's Tavern was on the Dartmouth side, a hundred yards up from the beach. They were sure Coleman was among the Dartmouth settlers escaping the French soldiers and Mi'kmaq warriors.

Hemsley and Wiseman stumbled to a nearby jetty, stole a rowboat, and made for Dartmouth. In the glow of the burning buildings, they crawled through the scrub bushes until they reached Coleman's Tavern, where they helped themselves to nine gallons of rum, twelve gallons of strong beer, and half a pound of Bohea Tea. Then they rowed back to Halifax, and, accompanied by several of their closest friends, went on a two-week drunk.

And that's what got them caught by the provost marshal, and subsequently tried and convicted of stealing from John Coleman's Tavern. The judge went easy on them, however, sentencing them to thirty-nine lashes and two days in the pillory.

Perhaps the judge recognized Reuben Hemsley and Tom Wiseman for the courageous men they were. After all, they had ventured into a French and Mi'kmaq attack for the sake of drink. And if that ain't brave, nothing is!

TEMPORARY INSANITY

Gad Saunders was a friendly man with a broad smile. He opened his home in Shelburne, Nova Scotia, to anyone, particularly peddlers. Gad and his wife, Jubel, enjoyed the news and gossip a peddler brought. A frequent overnight visitor to the Saunders home was a peddler named John Williams.

On New Year's Day 1801, Williams celebrated with Gad and Jubel. They ate a pork dinner and shared a jug of rum. At Williams's encouragement, Gad drank a lot more than his share of rum and retired to bed early. About midnight, he woke with a mouth as dry as a wool shirt. He went to the kitchen for water, and saw Jubel and John Williams snuggling before the fire, deeply engaged in "intimate conversation."

Gad flew into a rage. He chased Williams from the house, then turned on his wife. He called her a bitch, and with a two-bit axe, struck her three times—in the back, the shoulder, and the head. Then he pressed hot coals against her face and stuffed her body into the fireplace, only getting her halfway in before snuffing the fire.

Their twenty-year-old daughter found her mother in the fireplace early the next morning, and Gad in a drunken stupor on the floor beside her. Gad told his daughter what had happened and offered to build her a new house if she would not say a word. She fetched a magistrate.

Gad confessed to murdering his wife and to trying to burn away her shame and his crime. He was tried in Halifax, convicted, and sentenced to hang. While in jail awaiting execution, Gad regretted his crime, and in a petition to Governor John Wentworth, expressed his deep sorrow for the passionate rage that had erupted into a fit of violence and resulted in murder.

Chief Justice Blowers supported Gad's petition for a pardon. Blowers wrote the secretary of state in London, explaining that Saunders's conviction rested on the testimony of one witness (the daughter), and that the coroner's jury had not allowed a surgeon to examine the body. Blowers further stated that the condemned man "has been so contrite that a general compassion for him seems to prevail."

Governor John Wentworth also took an interest in Gad Saunders, and in March 1802, with the permission of the Colonial Office in London, pardoned Gad Saunders for the murder of his wife. The governor's reason was this: "...Gad Saunders seems to have acted under a derangement of mind and without premeditated malice or intentional murder."

This was the first known case in Maritime history of a murderer being pardoned on the grounds of "temporary insanity." Perhaps Governor John Wentworth sympathized with Gad Saunders's passionate rage. Perhaps the governor understood better than most how jealousy could fill one's mind and heart with violent intent. That's because the governor's wife, Lady Frances Wentworth, had a notorious reputation for engaging army and naval officers in "intimate conversation."

SHAVED TAILS

Discipline may well be the soul of an army, but too much discipline, particularly in a boarding school, can stir a brooding pot of boys to rebellion. That's what happened at King's College in Windsor, Nova Scotia, in 1793. King's was affiliated with the Anglican Church, and its students were expected to walk the straight and narrow.

President Porter made no attempt to spare the rod. Just the opposite: he kept a dozen alder switches at the ready, should any of the upper-class boys at King's College get out of line. One blow was never enough. In President Porter's mind, red welts on the back and buttocks were the true measure of effective punishment for recalcitrant students. When a beating wasn't enough, Porter forced students to drop to their knees and pray for hours.

In the fall of 1793, a few students got even. With a horn full of gunpowder, they blew apart the front porch of the president's house.

"Rebellion!" President Porter cried.

So serious was Porter's outcry that Charles Inglis, Anglican bishop of Nova Scotia, travelled from Halifax to investigate.

Bishop Inglis rode his prize horses to Windsor, trading one for the other every five miles. He arrived late at night and went straight to bed.

He woke the next morning and, after a hearty breakfast and before initiating his investigation, went to the stable to see to the care of his horses. What he saw left him speechless. The manes of his horses had been sheared and the tails completely shaved. The outrage against the lord bishop shocked the King's College faculty and the town. President Porter offered a reward for the names of the culprits.

Despite the president's heavy-handed use of all twelve of his alder switches, not a student squealed.

Many years later, several of New Brunswick and Nova Scotia's governing aristocracy were in Fredericton for a social affair. A few were discussing this prank on the lord bishop of Nova Scotia when Amos Botsford, a member of the provincial legislature, remarked to Doctor G. D. Fraser, "Of course, it will never be known who did it, but it has always been a wonder to me that the grey mare did not kick your brains out."

TWO STRIKES

During the eighteenth century in the Maritimes, there were no third-time criminal offenders. Two strikes and you were out. Criminals convicted of manslaughter, thieves, pickpockets, even burglars had one chance to change their lives, or the law would make certain they had no life to change.

In Halifax in October 1767, William Taylor stood before the court on a charge of theft. He had lifted two pennies' worth of soap from Malachi Salter's house.

Taylor offered no defence. He'd stolen the soap, and said so. Because this was Taylor's first offence, the judge leaned across the bar and sentenced Taylor to thirty-nine stripes on his naked back and to be branded with the letter "T" in the fat of his left hand. The "T" was for "thief."

Thirty-nine stripes, or forty less one, was a punishment pure and simple. It comes from the Book of Deuteronomy: "Forty stripes he may give him, and not exceed: lest, if he should exceed, and beat him above these with many stripes, then thy brother should seem vile unto thee."

The branding with the letter "T" or "M" (for "manslaughter") was more than just punishment. It was a paperless way of keeping score.

After the whipping and branding, Taylor made his way to the nearest grog shop to drink away the pain. Curiosity seekers paid for his drinks in exchange for a long look at the seared letter in his thumb.

Soon enough, Taylor was back on the street to work out the winter heaving and hauling cargo on the waterfront. Then the work froze up and his money played out, and before spring 1768, William Taylor was back in court for stealing bread and molasses from John Grant's store.

Again Taylor offered no defence, except to excuse his bad behaviour on the grounds of being out of work and hungry. Again Taylor was convicted, and again the judge leaned across the bar to pass sentence.

"Hold up your hands," the judge ordered.

Taylor did as he was told. There on the fat of his left hand was the white scar of his previous offence.

"That's two with you," the judge said, as he donned the black cap for passing a sentence of execution.

Bill Taylor now had two ends and the middle of a bad lot. His next stopping place was the gallows. On May 2, 1768, with two strikes against him (stealing bread and stealing soap), William Taylor was hanged.

John Smith had a name shared by many, and when he went to trial in 1771 for housebreaking, his common name almost did him in.

There was no doubt that he was guilty. He had been caught red-handed crawling from a back window in a house on Hollis Street in Halifax. After confessing to the crime in court, he begged the judge for the "benefit of clergy." This was a legal carry-over from the Middle Ages, when the law granted mercy to clergy convicted of a crime. Centuries later, this benefit was extended to anyone who could read Latin, because it was assumed only the clergy could do so. Then, years after that, anyone who could recite in Latin a memorized sentence received the benefit, and soon after that, first-time offenders who simply stood in court and asked for the benefit of clergy, whether or not they could read or recite Latin, had their sentences reduced.

When John Smith asked the court for the benefit, the judge shook his head. The name "John Smith" was familiar enough to the judge, and he remembered on two previous occasions convicting thieves named John Smith. The judge donned the black cap and sentenced Smith to death.

Smith went wild. He cried out that there was no such record for him, and held up his hands to prove it. A bailiff examined Smith's hands and informed the court that there was no scar on either of them.

"There will be now," the judge said, and commuted Smith's sentence of death to being burnt in the palm of his left hand, nine months in jail, and two years' parole.

John Smith heaved a sigh of relief. It could have been worse, much worse—and just for sharing the same name as two other thieves.

THE ITCH FOR GOLD

The five began digging a tunnel. Night after night, and as quietly as they could, they spit dirt and dug until daylight. George Bulger pointed the way. The lantern he held paled by comparison to the fire in his eyes. Bulger had seen Captain Kidd's gold in a dream. He knew where it was buried, and the four others believed him.

Bulger was six, maybe seven years old when he first heard the legend about Captain Kidd's gold from his father. The pirate had been running from a British man-of-war when he sailed his Jolly Roger into thick fog on the Bay of Chaleur. The next day, the fog lifted and the man-of-war was gone. Still, Kidd feared capture, and so sailed half a mile up the Miramichi River. He and some of his crew put ashore and trekked in from the beach, where they dug near a running brook and in the shadow of a big rock.

After burying the treasure, Captain Kidd drew his cutlass and, calling upon the darkness as his witness, cursed all those who would dig for it. Then he drove his cutlass straight into the heart of one of the sailors, who screamed at the stabbing and dropped on the beach as dead as dead. There the pirates left the sailor's body and bones to guard Captain Kidd's treasure.

That story had burned itself into George Bulger's mind. He talked about it every chance he got. His eyes would glaze over as he spoke, and his hands would fidget as though he were fingering the gold and jewels in the treasure chest. One night he dreamed about it. To hear him tell it, the dream was real, and he was there, watching Kidd and his crew digging in the moonlight that slanted over the water and gleamed like metal. He saw the big rock and the running brook, and heard the stab of shovels and the grunt of men heaving dirt into a pile at the edge of a big hole. He saw it all that night, and when he woke up, he remembered every detail and could walk straight to the place where he had seen Captain Kidd burying the treasure.

Bulger and his pals started digging at the side of a gully that drained spring runoff from a road to an oil slick pond that was overgrown with cattails. Bulger swore the running gully was the brook he had dreamed about, and that among the backfill of stone from the quarry was the big rock. On that first night, Bulger walked up and down the gully, perplexed about where to stab a shovel into the ground. Then he pointed, and said, "There!" and his four friends dug and dug.

They dug for four hours, non-stop and straight ahead like miners, clawing out the dirt and gravel, and boulders the size of a man's chest. They did not timber up the tunnel walls and roof because each night Bulger said the gold was just out of reach, six inches, maybe ten. He said he could feel it itching on his fingertips. Bulger kept pointing, and his pals kept digging.

For nearly a week, mysterious lights and ghostly sounds coming from a certain patch alarmed those living along the road between Newcastle and Chatham, New Brunswick, in Northumberland County. They heard the scraping of shovels on gravel, and low voices, one of them "goddamning" this and "jesuschristing" that. About the sixth night, one of the residents telephoned a judge to complain and woke the judge out of a sound sleep. The judge did the same to the Chatham chief of police, and the chief and two officers drove out to the Chatham highway to investigate.

The police saw a light flash in the roadside gully up ahead and then disappear. They stopped where they thought the light had been, climbed out of the cruiser, and stood and listened to voices which strangely seemed to come from beneath the centre line of the highway. The chief stayed with the cruiser while the officers scrambled down to the gully and beamed a flashlight into a twenty-foot-long tunnel. There were five men inside the tunnel. Two were digging the face wall and filling gunny sacks held by two others. The fifth held a lantern and directed the digging.

According to the police report and the *Fredericton Daily Gleaner,* the two diggers and two sack-holders went peaceably with the officers without complaint. George Bulger was another matter. Bulger refused to leave the tunnel. He hissed and spat at the officers when they came in to get him, and for the entire ride in a paddy wagon to the Chatham lockup, he fussed and fumed that he was within six inches of finding Captain Kidd's gold.

It took a trial judge to bring George Bulger to his senses. Bulger promised to fill in the diggings and to give up treasure hunting on the Chatham highway. Bulger kept his promise, though for a long time after, he swore he could still feel the itch of gold on his fingertips and see in the fullness of his dream the place where Captain Kidd had hidden his treasure.

MILITARY MISBEHAVIOUR

In those early years in Halifax, living next door to the British army was both a blessing and a curse. A blessing because they provided a formidable defence against French and Mi'kmaq attack. A curse because the soldiers bullied the townsfolk, harassed the ladies, and ran wild at night on drunken sprees of pillaging and vandalism.

Robert Grant was an original settler, and in 1752, he built a small house for his family in the north end of the settlement. He defined his property with a four-foot wooden fence.

That winter, soldiers from the North Barracks pulled down Robert Grant's fence and used it for firewood. Grant rebuilt the fence, and the following year the soldiers tore it down. Grant's complaints to the regimental officers fell on deaf ears.

In 1755, a gang of soldiers tore down John Scott's entire house and again used it for firewood. Scott and his family were inside when it happened. The homeowner could identify the soldiers easily enough, and was able to charge the culprits and have them brought to trial.

The soldiers' excuse was that they were cold and unwilling to venture into the woods to chop firewood for themselves. The Court of General Quarter Sessions sentenced them to be publicly whipped, but Governor Charles Lawrence, a military man, remitted their sentence.

In 1761, one hundred Haligonians sectioned off 1,500 acres in the north suburbs and built houses and outbuildings for their farms. The following year, soldiers ransacked the entire area. They stole everything in sight and tore down nearly forty houses for firewood. Again the soldiers went unpunished.

One wonders whether Halifax settlers would have been better off simply raising a white flag and surrendering their settlement to the enemy.

RUNAWAY FREIGHT TRAIN

(BJG)

To witnesses along that New Brunswick rail line, the speed reached by the freight train was beyond belief.

On Saturday, April 23, 1910, a CPR freight train left Edmundston for Woodstock, New Brunswick. Two men from Woodstock were in the cab—William Johnston, engineer, and Roy Craig, fireman.

All went well until the train reached Perth Junction. That was when two brakemen riding in the caboose noticed something peculiar. The rail line had steep grades, and on those going up, the engine had barely enough steam to make it, while on those going down, it rolled along at an alarming speed.

Hand over hand on the grab rails, the brakemen made their way forward over the catwalks. On reaching the cab, they found Johnston and Craig so drunk they could scarcely talk.

Now the train was picking up speed—and up ahead was a bend where the track followed the St. John River. The brakemen saw disaster unless they did something right away.

With the engineer and fireman too drunk to help, the brakemen nervously fiddled with the levers. Still the train picked up speed. At last, the brakemen pulled the brake and pushed back the throttle—and brought the train safely into Woodstock.

The case was the first of its kind to come before a New Brunswick court, and the court took the unauthorized drunken celebration seriously. The culprits, Johnston and Craig, each paid a fifty-dollar fine and spent three months in jail.

The heroes of the event, however, went unnoticed, their names not even reported by the local newspaper. They were simply two New Brunswick brakemen who risked their lives to stop a runaway train.

GALLOWS DAY

Gala and gallows are two disparate words that, strangely, have something in common. During earlier centuries in the Maritimes, gallows day, which was often held on market day, was a day when country folk came to town to socialize with friends and relatives. It was something of a festive, or gala, occasion. Of course, on gallows day, they also came to town to watch the hangings.

Because an execution was a public spectacle, it had a certain amount of pomp and circumstance. It often took on the appearance of a dramatic performance: the slow, plodding march to the gallows, the hesitant climb up the scaffold, a minister's prayers and exhortations, the last words of the condemned.

And some criminals treated their execution as an actor might treat his last performance. Michael McComb, in Saint John, was sentenced to death for murder, and showed no signs of being affected by the sentence.

On April 13, 1814, a large crowd gathered outside the jailhouse to watch him hang. McComb laughed and joked with the spectators on his way to the gallows. He practically pranced up the steps. He thanked the Baptist missionary, Mr. Reis, for his trouble. Then he nodded to the hangman that he was ready, and left this world smiling.

In 1816, in Halifax, Francis Roseman, another murderer, was just the opposite. Roseman had shot and killed Sergeant William Frederick outside the South Barracks in Halifax. On October 14, 1816, a Monday, he went to the gallows kicking and clawing. He refused to pray, and spent his last words cursing those who had sentenced him to death. However, when the hangman grabbed the rope and readied to give it a yank, Roseman shook his head, looked at the spectators, and said: "Oh well, here we go!"

NEW BRUNSWICK FEUD

(BJG)

French Lake is a pretty community in western Sunbury County, New Brunswick. In 1785, the Crown granted Elias Foss a fair chunk of the land there, in thanks for his service during the Revolutionary War. Foss lived to a ripe old age, and so long as he was alive, all was well. But when he died in 1842, all hell broke loose. Elias willed half his land to his son Charles and half to his daughter Caroline—adjacent properties, which made them neighbours.

Because there was so much land, most of it unused, Elias had never exactly marked off the property line between the two halves, and that's where the trouble started. The vague boundary made bad blood between Charles and Caroline. They stopped speaking.

Charles married Sarah Ann Moore, and she and Caroline spoke to each other—often, loudly, and using language a clergyman would not approve of. One day in 1887, the pair met on Lake Road. It was early spring, for the freshet had left the road littered with driftwood, and Sarah Ann (age fifty) and Caroline (age sixty-three) each grabbed a driftwood club and went at it.

They battered each other unmercifully. The younger woman beat her opponent till she lay helpless on the road, where a passerby found her. He brought a horse-drawn drag (sometimes called a stoneboat wagon) and pulled the half-dead Caroline home.

That beating settled nothing. It only made things worse. For a century, and at least four generations of Fosses, the feud went on—over some low-lying scrubland that no one really wanted.

HARBOURING DESERTERS

Mary Irwin was a raggedly dressed woman who lived on the outskirts of Halifax, Nova Scotia. Most neighbours thought she was a poor and lonely spinster, a woman who begged for her supper and crawled from her cold, empty bed at night to huddle in the chimney corner for warmth.

Little did they know that Mary Irwin seldom wanted for the company of a man, and that her poverty was a bluff to keep her neighbours from nosing into her business. That was because Mary did a regular trade in trafficking military deserters out of Nova Scotia.

In the eighteenth and early nineteenth centuries, a soldier's life was a miserable one. Order and discipline often came on the toe end of a boot or the business end of a cat-o'-nine-tails. And there were few volunteers. The military usually filled its ranks with criminals, or young men drafted off the streets and farms of Great Britain.

Mary Irwin provided these discontented soldiers with an easy means for desertion. She would quarter them in her house for several nights, until the coast was clear, then smuggle them on outgoing ships bound for New England or New York. They paid either in hard cash or with their military uniforms and equipment. Some even paid with the warmth of their company.

On February 4, 1825, after days of watching the comings and goings at Mary's house, the provost marshal raided the premises and discovered a deserter hiding in a chimney vent. He found the backroom stocked floor to ceiling with military belts, coats, tunics, and boots. From the amount of clothing and paraphernalia, it was obvious Mary Irwin had been in business for a long time. She certainly was not a poor woman, and judging by the number of soldiers who had passed through her door, she had not been a lonely one.

MISPECK MURDERS

Robert MacKenzie lived on the Mispeck Road, ten miles from Saint John, New Brunswick. He was a master tailor, a wealthy man.

Patrick Slavin, a neighbour, and Hugh Breen, MacKenzie's hired hand, often wondered about MacKenzie's gold—how much he had, where he kept it. At night, over a bottle of rum, they often talked about it. Another rum, and the talk got wild.

"Steal it!" Breen would urge. "We'll go to his house and steal it!"

October 24, 1857, was a cool autumn night. Slavin, Breen, and Slavin's eldest son, an imbecile who would do whatever his father said, knocked at MacKenzie's door.

From the window, Robert MacKenzie saw and recognized his hired hand. He opened the door and stepped into the night. Young Slavin moved from the shadows and, like a skilled woodsman, laid a broadaxe to MacKenzie's back. They then burst into the house, mad for money and blood. Young Slavin howled and flailed the axe. First MacKenzie's wife and then his four children were all cruelly butchered. The trio then ransacked the rooms for the gold, and set the house on fire.

Fire or no, neighbours suspected murder. When MacKenzie's dog turned up walking from woods covered in blood, they knew for certain. Fingers pointed at Slavin and Breen.

The murderers ran for St. Stephen and the Maine border, frantic through the brush and bogs. They were less than one hundred yards from the St. Croix River bank when a sheriff's posse nabbed them.

Breen hanged himself in jail. People complained he had cheated the gallows, but what they really meant was that he had cheated them from watching him swing. Young Slavin, because of his youth and mental health, received life in prison. Patrick Slavin, the father, begged forgiveness for his many sins, then stepped forward from the gallows and hanged.

ISRAEL OAKES

By 1816, the name Israel Oakes brought fear to travellers along the public roads between Halifax and Digby. Israel Oakes was a highway robber. Some embellished his reputation by describing Oakes as a Robin Hood or Dick Turpin (England's famous highway robber), because the Nova Scotia bandit made only the wealthy "stand and deliver."

There was some practical criminal sense to that. In those days, common travellers had little to steal. Wealthy merchants and the Royal Mail were where the money was.

Oakes was twenty-one years old, with a temper like a bobcat. He carried four pistols—two for firing when he rose from ambush, and two for threatening his victims with an early grave. His sidekick's name was Ebenezer Gaskill, a little man with a lame right arm.

So long as Israel Oakes stuck to highway robbery, there were few in the surrounding countryside who would turn him in. But the day he levelled his pistols at Edward Steel and fired point blank into Steel's chest, the whole of Annapolis Valley was out to get him.

The police dodger described Israel Oakes as "5'8" black eyes, dark hair, dark complexion, round face, scar on his upper lip, bow legged, stout made, a native of Nova Scotia, with a recent sword wound the length of his head." He was last seen on January 18, riding a black horse on the Cobequid Road heading out of the province.

On January 24, Saint John police caught him boarding a ship bound for Boston. They returned him to Annapolis Royal for trial.

As he walked from the courthouse toward the gallows on that cold, snowy morning, people no longer saw him as Robin Hood or Dick Turpin. They now recognized Israel Oakes for what he was—a murderer and a common thief.

EXECUTION OF CHARLES DEVERETT

On a wet April night in 1816, near the Presbyterian meeting house in Halifax, Captain John Westmacott, while making garrison rounds, spotted two men carrying a large sack between them. Thieves!

Westmacott reined his horse, and ordered the two men: "Stand to!"

There was a quick movement in the shadows. As Westmacott drew his sabre, the two men pulled him from his horse, clubbed him senseless, and stabbed him with his own sword. Then they ran for it, leaving behind the sack, which contained a few dozen mackerel they had stolen from Richard Tremaine's store.

Captain John Westmacott was a ranking officer in His Majesty's army and well connected within the halls of power in Great Britain. His brother, Richard, was a famous sculptor in London. John had been a gifted architect and had won a gold medal for his architectural design at the Royal Academy. He had served under Wellington during the Napoleonic War, using his artistic skill to sketch enemy positions.

The Nova Scotia government knew there would be hell to pay if it failed to bring Westmacott's murderer or murderers to justice. The governor of Nova Scotia immediately offered a reward of two hundred pounds for information that would lead to a successful capture and prosecution. It was more than enough money to make tongues wag. One wagging tongue belonged to James Flemming, a vagabond and petty thief.

With his hand open for the money, Flemming blabbed the names of Mike McGrath, a known plug-ugly in town, and Charlie

Deverett, an eighteen-year-old boy who admired McGrath's bullying behaviour. They were privates in the 64th Regiment stationed on Melville Island in Halifax.

Flemming claimed the two had sold him mackerel that night and promised to return with more of the same. A few hours later, around 3:00 AM, they returned empty-handed. When Flemming asked about the mackerel, McGrath said they had met an officer on grand rounds and had "done his business." The officer was "saucy," McGrath explained, "damned saucy, and got what he deserved."

Flemming's testimony was all the evidence the Crown had or needed. The attorney general opened the trial by saying the accused had killed "an officer they knew to be on duty with no visible pecuniary gain or future benefit. They had committed murder out of sheer cruelty."

The jury convicted the two men in ten minutes, and the judge sentenced them to hang on the following Monday between 10:00 AM and 2:00 PM. McGrath hardly blinked at the sentence of execution. Then he stood and admitted to the court that he and Deverett had committed robbery that night, but that he alone had done the killing.

Charles Deverett broke down in tears, swearing over and over that he was innocent.

The *Acadian Recorder* described the execution. On July 20, hanging day, at 2:00 PM, McGrath climbed the gallows in silence, while Deverett continued to assert his innocence. "The Executioner, who it was said was a female in disguise, bungled the job. The Executioner pulled out the wedge that held up the platform. It fell, leaving McGrath writhing in the agonies of death."

Deverett, however, fell with the platform to the ground below. His rope had broken.

There was wild confusion. Spectators called it a sign from God that Deverett was truly innocent, and they called for his immediate release. Legal minds argued that the sentence had specified execution between 10:00 AM and 2:00 PM. Since it was now past 2:00 p.m., Deverett was legally dead.

It took an hour and a half for the authorities to consider the matter. Then, at 3:30 PM, the court and the Executive Council denied the call for mercy and pronounced that justice must be done.

Charles Deverett retraced his steps to the gallows. The executioner cut a length of rope from that which had hanged McGrath. The whole time, Deverett had to watch the hangman cut the rope and tie a noose. Then the hangman slipped the noose over the condemned man's head, and launched young Charles Deverett into the everlasting.

FLINGING DIRT

On the night of May 4, 1911, William Molyneaux stood in the sheriff's office at Georgetown, Prince Edward Island, with his face twisted in shock. Sweat soaked his clothes from the four-and-half-mile run from his farm. "My wife," Molyneaux gasped, "killed herself." Then his legs buckled from exhaustion and he collapsed to the floor.

The sheriff rode out to Molyneaux's farm. In the summer kitchen, he found the woman suspended from a crossbeam. Her eyes bulged and her jaw hung open to her chest. He saw bruises on her legs where Molyneaux had tried to lift her body to slack the rope, until he realized she was dead. At least, that's how the sheriff figured it had happened, and that's what Molyneaux later confirmed.

Molyneaux said he had been ploughing a back field all day. When he returned to the house for a bite to eat, there she was dangling in the summer kitchen.

"Suicide," the sheriff wrote in his casebook, pure and simple.

And then about a week later, Molyneaux's eight-year-old son entered the sheriff's office. The boy had a different story to tell. He said his mother and father had been yelling at one another all that day, and that his father had never gone out ploughing. Instead, the boy's old man had sat on the back step, flinging dirt at the chickens and cursing under his breath. The boy also said that around suppertime he heard his mother screaming from the summer kitchen, and saw his father come out of the pantry just after her crying had stopped.

The sheriff rode back out to Molyneaux's farm and arrested William Molyneaux for the murder of his wife. It was during the ride out that the sheriff realized the bruises on the woman's legs were not from Molyneaux raising her body to slack the rope, but hauling down to stretch it.

TEA SMUGGLING

The Maritime provinces have long been famous for smuggling. Today, smugglers use the ragged coast to illegally import cigarettes and drugs. In centuries past, it was food, guns, and a lot of booze. In the 1840s, the hottest article smuggled into New Brunswick was tea. And the number one smuggler in those days was an adventurous horseman named Harry Dibble.

Of course, there were other, more professional smugglers than Harry Dibble. Two Americans in Hardscrabble, Maine, and an old

Irishman on the Houlton Road outside Woodstock, New Brunswick, had a regular back-and-forth trade that escaped the eyes of the customs officers for many years. But their system of bribes and kickbacks lacked the excitement of Harry Dibble's daring rides across the border.

Mounted on a roan horse, Harry crossed into Maine around Canterbury or Limerick. Then he would make for Houlton, where he stuffed his saddlebags full of rich Bohea Tea.

In those days, the British had a monopoly on the tea business in the colonies, and American tea was contraband. The British levied a twenty-five-cent tax on a pound of tea bought in Upper and Lower Canada and the Maritimes, and that made smuggled American tea a whole lot cheaper; and for Harry Dibble, well worth the risk.

Harry was no hide-and-seek smuggler who secretly slipped back and forth across the border under cover of darkness. No, Harry returned to New Brunswick on horseback in broad daylight, and usually with a half-dozen customs officers giving chase. He thought nothing of jumping the customs gate at a full gallop and in a hail of bullets.

Some say Harry Dibble smuggled just for the fun of it. And others say he made himself a fortune selling U.S. tea in New Brunswick. However it was, Harry Dibble was never caught, and until the Brits lifted the tax on tea, he continued his adventures in the smuggling game.

NEW BRUNSWICK KLAN

(BJG & BK)

On November 25, 1922, the Reverend Oscar Haywood of New York announced the Ku Klux Klan's expansion into Canada.

In the United States, the Klan was founded shortly after the Civil War. Its avowed purpose was to keep in place "uppity negroes" and their sympathizers. Its methods were based in fear—reinforced with beatings and even murder.

The base and fortress of the Ku Klux Klan in Canada was in New Brunswick. The hooded society in New Brunswick publicly burned crosses against the French and Roman Catholics, and anyone who offended its rigid rules of morality. Its New Brunswick nucleus seems to have formed around railway workers in the Centreville area of Carleton County. They soon acted.

On a February night in 1925, the Klan took the law into their own hands, and raided and put out of business eight Woodstock houses suspected of being dens of bootleggers and prostitutes. That caught the attention of many New Brunswickers who wanted strict regulation of morality. The ranks of the New Brunswick Klan swelled. Soon its adherents appeared on the side of law and order in York County, Sunbury, Queens, Kings, and Westmorland near the Nova Scotia border.

The New Brunswick Klan was also outraged at the growing influence of the French and Roman Catholics. To make their point, they burned fiery crosses on the river ice in Fredericton in 1927, in Shediac in 1928, and in 1930 at the farm of a man named Wilbern near Moncton.

In 1927, the school trustees at Rough Waters, Northumberland County, hired Miss P. Manville as their schoolteacher. Miss Manville was a Roman Catholic. Within days, the trustees got an order from the Klan to mend their ways. The Klan complained that this teacher not only taught Roman Catholic catechism in her school, but also taught the French language three times per week and English only twice. The School Trustees fired Miss Manville.

In 1931, the New Brunswick Klan feigned respectability and incorporated itself as The Beaver Society. They then tried to stop Allison Dysart of Kent County from becoming premier. Dysart was Roman Catholic. A Ku Klux Klan circular pronounced: "If Dysart is elected, Rome will rule!"

Murders are hard to prove, but in 1927, some say New Brunswick's Ku Klux Klan murdered a man. His name was Edward Armstrong from Perth, Victoria County. The sixty-four-year-old farmer had favoured a Francophone, Avard DeMerchant, over an Anglophone for a job on his farm. A few days later, December 28, 1927, he received a threatening letter from the local chapter of the Ku Klux Klan ordering him to fire the Frenchman and hire the Englishman. Armstrong refused. Days later he was found dead in his barn.

The *Telegraph-Journal* from Saint John, New Brunswick, reported the killing. Neighbours had found Edward Armstrong's body in the barn under a pile of hay. His head was smashed into an unrecognizable mass of flesh and bone, his nose was crushed into his face and his upper lip was forced back, while one eye was completely gouged out of its socket.

Captain E. C. P. Salt of the New Brunswick Provincial Police investigated, but no one was charged with the murder of Edward Armstrong. The case is still an unsolved murder.

It has been said the Klan's leaders were men in high places. Perhaps that's why the hate-mongering members of the Invisible Empire who once threatened New Brunswick's way of life were never punished.

JIM AND BUCK

A large crowd gathered at the Moncton railway station. Many had travelled from outlying districts to get a close-up look at the prisoner—a bandit and cop killer the press called "Jim." A few months before, these same people were not so brave. During the fall of 1892, Jim and his partner, "Buck," had terrorized the countryside from Moncton, New Brunswick, to Pictou, Nova Scotia.

Jim and Buck were bandits who robbed banks, stores, and farmhouses at gunpoint. The Moncton police had been chasing them for months. But it seemed the boys knew the backcountry roads as well as the locals, or had locals hiding them out.

On August 1, 1892, Joe Steadman, a Moncton cop, had Jim and Buck trapped in a house on the outskirts of Moncton. The boys blasted their way out, and Steadman went down with a .32 calibre slug in his heart.

That brought on the largest manhunt in New Brunswick's history, and a reward of $750. Money has a way of changing one's perspective on things, a way of altering attitudes. If anyone had been hiding the boys or guiding them over backcountry roads, they soon stopped. And in a matter of days, the cops caught Buck near Amherst, Nova Scotia. He said his real name was Robert Olsen, and that he was too drunk to shoot straight the night Joe Steadman took a bullet in the chest.

Jim remained on the run, making his way to Bass River, Nova Scotia, where he broke into the farmhouse of Mrs. Simpson and stole food. News of the robbery reached Peter Carroll, a policeman from Pictou.

It had rained the night before the robbery, and when Carroll arrived in Bass River, he found footprints in the mud and tracked them for more than a mile to the farmhouse of Robert Carter. Pete Carroll boldly entered the Carter kitchen and squared off against the outlaw named Jim. The farmer sat at a table between outlaw and cop. Then Carroll opened his coat to show he was unarmed. At that, Jim reached in his pocket for his .38, a "Boston Bulldog." Before he could draw and aim, Carroll laid him cold with a solid right to the jaw.

Carroll returned Jim to Moncton for trial. On the way, Jim begged Pete Carroll to shoot him dead, because he was afraid to go to the gallows for Joe Steadman's murder.

But that was not how it played out. Robert Olsen was the one who faced the charge of murder. He had been carrying a .32 calibre pistol when he was caught and arrested,

Robert Olsen hanged for Steadman's murder. Jim got twenty-five years for numerous counts of robbery. Several newspaper reporters considered the hanging of Robert Olsen a miscarriage of justice. While awaiting trial, Jim told one of these reporters that he had always carried two guns, a .38 and a .32 calibre. He had ditched the .32 when he read in the newspaper about the gun that killed Steadman.

He never did tell the court his real name, and he went to prison known only by the name of "Jim." And it was by that name that he finally made a public confession. "I hereby state in the presence of witnesses that I fired the shot from a .32 calibre pistol which killed Joseph E. Steadman on the night of August 1, 1892."

SAMUEL ISLES

Gorham's Rangers were a wild bunch. They were a vicious, bloodthirsty lot of scalp hunters comprised of hooligans, criminals, and the offscourings of the colonies. The British army kept them around solely because they were good fighters. In 1751, the greatest threat to the new settlement of Halifax came from the French and the Mi'kmaq.

When Gorham's Rangers were not fighting the enemy, they were fighting among themselves or with other regiments. Their commanding officers, Captain Charles Proctor and Captain Clapham, often turned a blind eye to the disorder and outright hooliganism of these men.

On September 11, 1751, Samuel Isles, a member of Gorham's Rangers, took his commanding officer at his word. On that night, Joseph Payne returned to the barracks drunk, belligerent, and boisterous. Captain Clapham was himself a little drunk, and ordered Samuel Isles to shut up Payne any way he could.

Instinctively, Isles followed the violent ways of his Ranger regiment. He tried to punch Payne unconscious. He broke Payne's nose. Still Payne continued hollering and making a racket. Isles then tied Payne to a chair, jammed a drummer's stick sideways in Payne's mouth, and gagged him with a length of cloth.

That did it. Isles went to Captain Clapham's quarters to report that Payne was well under control. When he returned to the barracks, Payne was dead. He had suffocated from the broken nose and gag.

Isles now faced a charge of murder. At his trial, Captain Clapham came to his defence, insisting that Isles had only taken orders to the extreme. The court agreed, reduced the charge to manslaughter, and sentenced Isles to be branded on the hand with the letter "M."

TWO WOMEN AND A NOOSE

Martha Orphin holds the dubious distinction of being the first woman hanged in early Halifax. In the spring of 1760, she drew a long-bladed knife on Robert Hemmings, slashed him once, then drove the blade through his breastbone and into his heart. She was tried for murder, convicted, and sentenced to hang.

On May 20, the jailer led her to the foot of George Street, where a crowd had gathered to watch the spectacle. Martha climbed into the back of a dray cart. The hangman set the noose, and the cart drove away, leaving Martha Orphin behind, dangling about two feet off the ground.

Martha Orphin went to her execution quietly, though visibly shaken. Not so with Margaret Murphy.

Margaret Murphy was a regular Halifax hellcat. On October 18, 1791, Murphy picked a fight with Maria Ball. Murphy claimed Ball had stolen her man. They spit, scratched, bit, and punched. And when it was over, Maria Ball lay dead on the floor of Philpot's Boarding House. Murphy had strangled her.

On October 26, Margaret Murphy walked to the gallows quietly, her downcast eyes sneaking peeks at those who had gathered to watch her hang. No sooner had the executioner fitted the noose around her neck than a fierceness came over her face. She shook a clenched fist and cursed all within earshot. Then she spit on the spectators in the front ranks, laughed madly, and called for the hangman to get on with it.

He did, hoisting her nearly to the cross spar, where Margaret Murphy dangled for more than an hour before a doctor declared her dead.

FLAT NOSE GEORGE CURRY

There are some people who see only the limitations to life on an island. They dwell upon the things they cannot do, instead of appreciating and making the most of what life on an island has to offer. And then there are those who leave the bellyaching and mollycoddling to others, and pack up and set off from the island to follow the career they set for themselves. One of the latter was a young man from Charlottetown, Prince Edward Island, by the name of George Curry.

George wanted to be a train robber, and he recognized almost at once that he would have a difficult time fulfilling that ambition on Prince Edward Island in the 1880s. So George Curry went west, where there was more opportunity to make a name at robbing trains. He started off robbing trains in Canada's west, but soon moved south of the border to the United States, where there were more trains and better pickings.

George got real good at robbing trains. There were wanted posters for him from Kansas to California. They pictured George as the ugly man he was, with his nose pressed flat against his face. The police dodger called him "Flat Nose George Curry." George didn't mind. His flat nose and ugly kisser made him more recognizable and feared when he boarded a train with his pistols drawn and cocked.

In the 1890s, Flat Nose Curry was a partner with Butch Cassidy and the Sundance Kid in the Hole in the Wall Gang, and they raised hell throughout the American West, robbing banks and trains.

The gang broke up in 1898. Cassidy and the Kid went to South America, where they were shot down in Bolivia. Flat Nose Curry made tracks for Utah. Here, in 1900, a posse ran him down and, in a hail of bullets, Flat Nose George Curry from Prince Edward Island fell dead.

PRISON BREAK

Joseph Bennett had a plan for escape from the moment he set foot in the Nova Scotia Penitentiary on Halifax's Northwest Arm. It was a daring plan, one that would take time to put into action.

In 1849, Bennett entered the Nova Scotia Penitentiary, and immediately ingratiated himself with the governor of the prison, Thomas Carpenter, a drunkard. Within a month, Bennett became a regular visitor at Carpenter's office. With each visit, Bennett brought a jug of rum acquired from friends on the outside.

Bennett then enlisted six other prisoners into his plan. They were a mix of thieves and murderers, all with experience at sea, and one of them, William Roach, was capable of piloting a ship to Boston without a compass.

On May 3, 1849, Bennett saw Governor Carpenter to bed in a drunken stupor. He then slipped the prison keys from a peg, sneaked past the guards, and quietly unlocked the cell doors of his inmate accomplices.

Within minutes, and with outside assistance, they were across the Northwest Arm and aboard a two-mast sloop, with sails billowing in a strong breeze. However, once the sloop cleared Halifax Harbour, Bennett's leadership and plan evaporated. The escaped convicts argued about their destination. Bennett and Roach opted for the safety and the freedom of the open sea; the others wanted to sail the coastline along the southwest shore. Bennett and Roach were outvoted.

A few days later, near Lunenburg, the HMS *Daring* drew alongside the sloop and fired a round across the bow. The crew of the *Daring* boarded the sloop and arrested those on board. Bennett and Roach were not among them.

According to one of the captured prisoners, Bennett and Roach had lowered the jolly boat, rigged canvas, and sailed off on their own.

CON MAN

Tom Winters lied like truth, so much so that when he hit Halifax in March 1825, he had the Halifax business community believing every word he spoke.

But this was not the first time Winters had lied to Halifax's businessmen. Three years before, Winters had arrived in Halifax calling himself Thomas Wilson of the company Thompson & Wilson. And he had cheated several Halifax businessmen out of a lot of money. Now he was back with more schemes, more deals, and more lies.

Tom Winters told William Carritt, who owned a yard-goods store, that he had a load of cordwood bound for Halifax and that he was prepared to sell it cheap. Carritt agreed to buy, but refused to offer a down payment until the cordwood landed.

Winters had prepared for this. He produced a bill of exchange for goods he had sold to Mr. Leishman, another Halifax businessman. The bill of exchange for salted pork with Mr. Leishman was from Tom Winters's previous visit to Halifax. Nevertheless, the note served as proof of his good character, and it convinced Mr. Carritt to provide one hundred pounds as a down payment on the cordwood.

Tom Winters was now one hundred pounds richer with Carritt's money. However, on his way back to Leishman, to scheme him out of money with the bill of exchange he now held for Carritt, he was recognized by Thomas Bolten of Bolten's General Store. Bolten called the sheriff, who soon discovered that Tom Winters was indeed the man who had cheated several Halifax merchants three years before. And a Mr. Wilkie confirmed it. He said he had just loaned Tom Winters one shilling as down payment on a load of pork and mutton, and he admitted that he had done so despite being swindled out of three pounds by the same man three years before.

Another man Winters had previously cheated was none other than William Carritt, the dry goods merchant who had bought the cordwood.

One wonders at the gullibility of Halifax businessmen, and whether sharpers from New England saw a business trip to Nova Scotia as nothing short of taking candy from a baby.

DOWN WITH HANGING

During his trial, John Lee claimed a strange, uncontrollable urge had possessed him, like the sudden, overpowering temptation of the devil.

The prosecution said otherwise. The prosecution claimed John Lee had coldly calculated murder and highway robbery—and the Crown proved it.

John Lee and Thomas Trueman were day labourers in Hubbards, Nova Scotia. On Christmas Day in 1833, they walked to Halifax for the holidays. On the way, Lee asked to borrow three pounds from Trueman, and as Trueman opened his purse, Lee got a good look inside. At the old west gate to the city, near the Citadel, Lee slowed by a step or two, then grabbed Trueman from behind and ran a razor across Trueman's throat.

Lee's claim of sudden devilish possession was nonsense. About an hour after the incident, he sat in Franklin's Tavern, dining on beefsteak at Trueman's expense.

He was on his second helping when the door to Franklin's swung open and Thomas Trueman entered with two constables at either arm.

Lee's razor had cut through the knotted handkerchief around Trueman's neck, the stiffener, and the shirt collar, but only scratched Trueman's throat. Trueman's slump to the ground had been a faint.

At trial, Lee told the court that he was born in Rochester, New York, and until the age of twelve had lived in Chatham, Ontario, where his father apprenticed him to a Great Lakes fisherman. He served seven years in the fishing fleet, learning the ropes and working up his share of the catch. He soon made his way to the east coast, then shipped out on a merchant vessel bound for the Caribbean.

He sailed in and out of one hungry Caribbean port after another, until the sloop *Sapphire* sailed north to Lunenburg, Nova Scotia, where James Lee jumped ship. He knocked around the South Shore a bit, doing odd jobs along the waterfront. In Hubbards Cove, he went to work for the Dauphnee family, and that's where he met Thomas Trueman.

At this point, James Lee broke down crying, blubbering about having no cause for robbing and razoring Thomas Trueman, but swearing on all that was holy that the devil had a hand in his crime.

Unmoved by Lee's claim of devilish intervention, the jury convicted Lee in short order. His lawyer, Mr. Ritchie, appealed for mercy, but the judge offered none. Instead, the judge donned the black cap and sentenced James Lee to hang.

Despite Lee's obvious guilt, Reverend Cogswell raised a public outcry against Lee's execution. Cogswell wanted no more public hangings in Halifax. He insisted they provoked the animal instincts of the populace and whetted the public's appetite for violence. This may very well have been the first campaign against capital punishment.

Cogswell solicited public support and used the *Novascotian* newspaper to get his message out. He delivered a blow-by-blow account of Lee's remorse, and expressed the need for God's grace. The soul-saver described the condemned man as a hard worker who had lost his footing on the straight and narrow, and now, in his final days, was overwhelmed with sorrow.

Most Haligonians did not agree with Cogswell. They wanted a hanging, if not for justice's sake, then for its entertainment value.

And so on a cold February day in 1835, John Lee walked to the gallows, attended by Reverend Cogswell. Lee required help up the stairs, but composed himself once on the platform. Then he exhorted the hundreds of spectators to fear the Lord and mend their evil ways.

Many shouted him down, eager for the hangman to get on with his business.

The hangman placed a handkerchief in Lee's hand, then paused a moment as Lee and Cogswell together uttered one last prayer.

It would take many more years before the general populace would become sensitive enough to welcome legislative reform that would deprive them of the thrill and excitement they experienced at a public hanging. To Cogswell's credit, he gave the movement against capital punishment a head start.

FLAHAVEN MURDER

Charlotte Flahaven wanted her husband, John Flahaven, dead. Since the birth of their second daughter, the couple hardly spoke—except when they were arguing, and that was often. It was so often that Cape Bretoners regularly travelled for miles to drink at the couple's North Sydney tavern, just to watch the Flahavens shelling each other with torrents of verbal abuse.

Charlotte was the more disagreeable of the two. She was particularly disagreeable with the women of North Sydney. Charlotte did not like women, but she did like men. Charlotte liked men about as much as she liked money. She figured with her husband out of the way, she could have both.

In the summer of 1833, two sailors stayed overnight at Flahaven's Tavern. Their names were William Johnston and Reuben Easman. They were hard-weather men who drank and brawled and knew the business end of whatever weapon they happened to be carrying at the time.

Early the next morning, Easman woke John Flahaven to tell the tavern keeper that his ox had run off. Flahaven was up and out of the tavern on the fly, chasing the animal down a road no wider than a bridle path. At a turn in the road, Johnston was waiting for him. Easman followed close behind. Together, they killed John Flahaven with an axe.

They returned to the tavern and bragged to Charlotte about what they had done. From the conversation, there was no doubt Charlotte had planned the whole thing. At least, that's what Charlotte's oldest daughter said she heard through the walls of her bedroom.

Without her mother or the sailors knowing, the girl ran for Captain MacKinnon, the Justice of the Peace. Captain MacKinnon arrived at Flahaven's Tavern to find the sailors and Charlotte drinking, and thick in conversation. He arrested the sailors on the spot. He took the daughter at her word and arrested the mother as well. Then he used the Flahaven dog to find the body.

The sailors confessed, confirming the girl's testimony that Charlotte had instigated the whole affair.

In August 1833, Richard John Uniacke Jr., a justice of the Nova Scotia Supreme Court and on circuit in Cape Breton, presided at the murder trial. The jury took little time in finding Charlotte

Flahaven, William Johnston, and Reuben Easman guilty. And Justice Uniacke took even less time to sentence them to hang.

On September 19, 1833, men and women travelled from far and wide to North Sydney to watch the hanging. Most of the men regretted the loss of the continuous entertainment at Flahaven's Tavern. The women did not.

COUNTERFEITING

In 1757, when John Young entered a Halifax court under a charge of high treason, the one thing he had going for him was the seriousness of the charge.

John Young was a small-time counterfeiter. He had made nine pieces of eight (Spanish dollars) and ninety-nine pistareens (a coin valued at one-quarter an English shilling). Not a whole lot of money, but enough to get him hanged if convicted.

And that is what troubled the grand jury. The twelve men had a hard time charging John Young with high treason for what they considered a petty crime. But English law provided them with no way out. Counterfeiting any coin was high treason, no two ways about it.

The jury decided to erase the words "high treason" from the indictment, then returned a true bill against John Young.

The court was not to be fooled so easily. It quashed the indictment and drew up a new one, and boldly underlined the words "high treason." The grand jury fussed and fumed about sending a petty criminal and first-time offender to the gallows, and finally they agreed on a solution to their problem. Despite the solid evidence, the grand jury decided to not find a true bill against John Young, which meant the charge had to be dismissed.

This threw the Nova Scotia court into confusion. Chief Justice Jonathan Belcher blistered at the prospect of allowing a criminal to go free on a technicality. Belcher's solution was simple. He would guarantee the grand jury a pardon for John Young upon his conviction on a charge of high treason. This would uphold the law and spare the counterfeiter the gallows. The grand jury agreed.

John Young was subsequently convicted of high treason and immediately pardoned.

BENEDICT ARNOLD

Benedict Arnold is the most hated man in United States history. He betrayed his country to the British during the American Revolution. Today, his name is infamous. It means traitor, deceiver, backstabber.

After the American Revolution, in 1784, Benedict Arnold settled in New Brunswick on a land grant below Fredericton on the St. John River. He resided there for several years, and was disliked by New Brunswickers almost as much as he was by Americans.

Arnold was a quick-tempered, mean-spirited scoundrel, and no one knew that better than Nehemiah Beckwith, a shipbuilder on the St. John River near Jemseg.

Arnold contracted Beckwith to build a ship he intended to name *Lord Sheffield*. The written contract specified tonnage, dimensions, price, and time of delivery. Here, Arnold was a stickler.

He insisted on the builder's strict adherence to the deadline, or the ship would be forfeited to him. And he put it in writing.

Beckwith agreed to the terms. The time frame was well within reason, or so Beckwith thought.

Shortly before the launch date, Arnold made changes in the design. Beckwith argued that such changes would be impossible to complete on time. Arnold smiled and agreed to a two-week extension, and the men shook on it.

Soon after Nehemiah Beckwith delivered the ship, well within the two-week extension but past the first deadline, Arnold prosecuted the shipbuilder for violating the contract. Beckwith protested that they had extended the deadline to accommodate Arnold's design changes and shook on it.

A handshake? Arnold laughed at such a claim. In court, he denied there was a handshake and argued that the written contract should be upheld. The court ruled in favour of Benedict Arnold, and Nehemiah Beckwith was financially ruined.

THE PREACHER

For many early settlers, farming in Nova Scotia was a hardscrabble way of life, and anyone perceived as successful at it was inevitably believed to be hoarding gold. People thought that about Frederick Eminaud, who lived with his wife and an apprentice girl a mile and a half outside Lunenburg, Nova Scotia.

One day in late March 1791, an itinerant preacher stood before the charred remains of what had been Frederick Eminaud's log cabin. Only the chimney remained standing.

When the preacher found two bloodstained clubs on the ground outside the cabin and what looked like scuff marks from a body having been dragged into the building, he suspected someone had believed all the money talk and murdered Eminaud, along with Eminaud's wife and apprentice girl.

There was not much evidence for local authorities to go on. Then, a month later, Sheriff Robert Clark overheard loose talk in a Halifax tavern. George Boutilier said he and his brother John had come upon a sizable sum of money down in Lunenburg. George said they had found the stash on the side of a road, but Sheriff Clark suspected something else. He arrested the Boutilier brothers, shackled them in irons aboard the schooner *Diligent,* and delivered them to Lunenburg, where they were tried for the Eminaud murders.

Chief Justice Thomas Andrew Strange presided at the trial, along with Justice Brenton Haliburton. The only evidence against Fred and John Boutilier was the bloodstained clubs the preacher had found and the tavern talk. Yet the jury took little time in finding the Boutilier brothers guilty of murder.

Maybe it was grim intuition, but as it turned out, the jury was right.

After the Boutilier brothers had climbed to the gallows, George stepped forward and, before the hundred or so gathered for thespectacle, confessed to the murders. George and his brother had struck Eminaud down outside the barn. The wife and girl had responded to Eminaud's cry, and when they came from the house carrying a lantern, the Boutilier brothers killed them too.

George said all this with lowered head and teary eyes. Then he lifted his head and fixed his gaze on those watching from the front ranks, and said he had been moved to confess by the consoling words of the man who had administered to his and his brother's spiritual needs while they sat in jail, the same man who now stood beside them on the gallows—the preacher, the same preacher who had discovered the burned log cabin and bloodstained clubs.

THOMAS TREMLETT

It mattered little that Thomas Tremlett was not a lawyer and that he knew very little about the law. Governor Smith simply wanted to do a favour to get his old friend out of debt, and so Smith appointed Thomas Tremlett chief justice of Prince Edward Island.

Tremlett spent the next eleven years repaying the favour. His legal decisions always benefited the governor's friends. By 1815, merchants and landowners had had enough. They petitioned the governor to remove Tremlett from high office, charging the chief justice with three counts of promoting favouritism from the bench.

Tremlett answered each charge in a letter to the governor: "To the first charge, your Excellency, I answer that it is a lie. To the second charge, I say that it is a damned lie, and to the third charge that it is a damned infernal lie!"

Governor Smith accepted this as an appropriate defence and dismissed all charges against Tremlett.

Tremlett served as chief justice from 1813 to 1824. In all that time, except by the governor and his friends, not one good word was ever said about him. Because he was paid according to time spent presiding over a case, Tremlett dragged out proceedings that normally would be decided in a single day. In 1814, he sat fifty-two days to try twelve jury cases.

In 1824, a petition to the Colonial Office in London, England, succeeded in getting both Governor Smith and Tremlett relieved of their duties.

In his eleven-year stint as chief justice of Prince Edward Island, Thomas Tremlett proved one thing, and proved it well—one does not have to be a lawyer to manipulate the law for one's own good.

PICTOU CHARITY

On December 23, 1826, Jeremy Welson and a fourteen-year-old boy wandered into Pictou, Nova Scotia, wearing the telltale signs of sadness and misery. And they had a story to go with that tattered, woeful look.

"Shipwreck!" Jeremy Welson said. "Storm in the Gulf of St. Lawrence. We ran aground on Cape Breton Island, just north of Mabou."

He said they had sailed from the Miramichi in New Brunswick on the *Aberdeenshire* under Captain Oswald. Welson and the boy had made it to shore along with the first mate, but the captain and rest of the crew had drowned.

The mate had broken his thighbone, Welson said, so he and the boy had made a stretcher from driftwood and lugged the mate into Mabou, where he was now recovering. They had received the greatest kindness and charity in Mabou, Welson said. Now, with their strength restored, Welson and the boy were making their way back to the Miramichi—on foot. "We want nothing more to do with the sea."

The townsfolk in Pictou pitied these two shipwrecked sailors, and wanted to show themselves every bit as charitable as those in Mabou—maybe more so. Besides food and lodging, the townsfolk raised a sizable purse of money to pay the costs of travelling to the Miramichi.

Robert Dawson, a community leader, even wrote his condolences to the family of Captain Oswald. A return letter, however, said Captain Oswald was very much alive, and that the *Aberdeenshire* still lay at anchor in the harbour.

By this time, Welson and the boy had skedaddled, more than likely on their way to Halifax with their stomachs and pockets bulging on Pictou charity.

A STUBBORN MAN

Doctor Capel was so stubborn that despite the crying need for a medical man in his Southport, Prince Edward Island, community he refused to practice his profession. In years past, a fellow physician had snubbed him. To get even, Capel swore he would never doctor again—and he didn't.

He kept himself and his wife and family on the yearly remittance his relatives sent from England, most of which he spent on himself. While his wife and children dressed in rags and ate potatoes three times a day, he consumed copious amounts of alcohol.

A word of complaint from his wife, and Doctor Capel would fly into a rage and beat her severely. Then he would cut back on her allowance for food, and refuse to budge despite the hungry cries of his children.

At last, in 1864, his wife had had enough and filed for divorce on grounds of cruelty. The court easily ruled in her favour, and ordered Doctor Capel to pay her fifty dollars per year in alimony.

He stubbornly refused.

The court held him in contempt, and jailed him until he agreed to pay his wife the alimony. Still he refused, and sought release on a legal technicality. He lost the case, and again the court ordered him to remain in jail until he agreed to pay.

Doctor Capel declared in open court that he would rot in jail before he would give a single penny for his family's support.

He remained stubborn and hard-hearted to the end, and spent the rest of his life in jail, just as he said he would do.

TOM RAMSDEN, SMUGGLER

Smuggling between New England and Nova Scotia was a way of life in the eighteenth century, especially during the American Revolution. Officials on both sides of the border tried to stop it, but ended up with little or nothing to show for their efforts.

Tom Ramsden was a Boston smuggler. When his ship, the *Polly*, cleared customs as it sailed out of Boston Harbor, it had all the markings of a fishing vessel—bait, nets, and long lines. But as it crossed the Bay of Fundy, the *Polly* miraculously transformed into a trading ship. By the time it reached Nova Scotia's South Shore, Tom Ramsden and his crew had the *Polly* chockablock with merchandise and ready for business.

The decks were now laden with barrels and hogsheads of molasses, rum, and everything else Great Britain taxed heavily. Nova

Scotia coastal villages welcomed Ramsden and his crew with open arms. There was no sneaking in and out of coves and inlets under cover of darkness, not for Tom Ramsden. He traded by day. He dropped anchor in a harbour, announced his presence with a long trumpet blast, then waited for the boatloads of townsfolk to come clambering over the gunwales, their pockets filled with coin and their eyes a-goggle for cheap New England rum and untaxed finery.

In July 1886, Pat McDonnough, a tidewaiter (a sort of customs officer) at Shelburne, decided to take his job seriously. He boarded Ramsden's ship and marked the main mast with the King's Broad Arrow, the sign of a seized vessel.

Ramsden scratched his head and laughed at McDonnough's efforts to enforce the letter of the law. Then he appealed to two prominent Shelburne merchants, Jarvis and Thayer.

Within three months, Ramsden was once again trading smuggled goods from Canso to Yarmouth, and Pat McDonnough was unemployed. Shelburne merchants had petitioned the Nova Scotia government in Halifax to remove Pat McDonnough from his duties because he was unnecessarily pestering honest businessmen—like Tom Ramsden.

AN OLD OFFENDER

James Ryan was convicted of burglary on the Kingston Peninsula in New Brunswick and sentenced to hang. On that day in 1824, he climbed the gallows—his leg irons rattling with each step—and faced the mob of spectators below. He was hardly forty years old, his dark hair falling over one eye, his body hard and strong. A man in his prime, yet he seemed indifferent to death. His entire demeanour suggested that hanging would be a comfort. He was so composed, he even instructed the hangman as to how the rope should be strung.

He was given a last word to make amends for his crime before he met his maker. James Ryan made the most of the opportunity to speak.

He confessed to a string of crimes that reached from Fredericton to Saint John, New Brunswick, and on to Halifax, Nova Scotia, and back again. More than ten years of crime, and this was his first time caught. He had passed forged checks to Francis Stevens of Fredericton under the name John George Dunn; robbed a green grocer in Saint John; stolen from Simpson's Dry Goods Store in Dartmouth; passed forged currency to Marshall Story in Halifax; murdered a man at Nine Mile River in Nova Scotia; and broken into a house on the Kingston Peninsula, stolen a set of silver spoons, and had his way with the homeowner's wife.

James Ryan had committed more crimes, a lot more, but he seemed to run out of words to describe them. He looked the spectators over and asked their forgiveness, and said his real name was Thomas Quigley. Then he nodded to the hangman, and left this world with a wry smile and a pissing pair of breeches.

NEW BRUNSWICK'S FIRST MURDER

(BJG)

The unenviable distinction of being the first murderer in New Brunswick goes to a black woman named Nancy Mosely.

She lived with her husband, John, in Parr Town, now Saint John. John Mosely had served King George during the American Revolution, and so, like other Loyalists, received a grant of land in New Brunswick for his services.

Nancy was quiet and even-tempered. John was a bitter man, a grumbler who had little good to say about anyone or anything. When he took to drink, which he took to often, he was mean and belligerent.

Exactly what he did to Nancy on that morning of September 27, 1784, is lost to history, but whatever it was, it left Nancy in a rage. She banged out of their clapboard shanty to the barn and returned a moment later with an iron digging-fork.

One sharp blow to the side of his head was all it took. John Mosely was dead.

The grand jury presentiment read like this: "That Nancy Mosely, not having the fear of God before her eyes, but being moved and seduced by the instigation of the devil…did, wilfully, feloniously and of her malice aforethought, make an assault with an iron fork and struck John Mosely upon the head near unto the temple."

When she was brought into court, the charge was changed from murder to manslaughter. Her husband's bad temper had something to do with that. On February 1, 1785, the court convicted Nancy Mosely and sentenced her to be branded upon the left thumb with the letter "M." Her name was recorded in New Brunswick history as the province's first murderer.

ISLAND JUSTICE

A crime wave hit the small settlement of St. Eleanor's, Prince Edward Island. At night, thieves had the roads to themselves without fear of being run down by a sheriff, a magistrate, or any other lawman. That's because St. Eleanor's, like many Maritime towns, did not have a regular police force, and the only county sheriff was usually miles away.

In October 1867, townsfolk in St. Eleanor's had had enough of cowering in their homes at night with their hearts knocking their ribs, while thieves and riff-raff ran riot throughout the countryside. They formed a vigilance committee. Groups of seven men, armed with everything from pistols to pitchforks, patrolled the town streets and roads at night, calling to each other through the darkness, "All is well! All is well!"

One November night, the committee stumbled onto a thief helping himself to the cash register of a dry goods store in the upper end of town. Before they had time to worry about being afraid, they pounced on the thief with their cudgels and clubs.

The thief never knew what hit him. And what came next served notice to all thieves and riff-raff bent on plying their criminal trade in this small community: the people of St. Eleanor's had their own methods for administering justice.

The seven-man vigilance committee, which had now swelled to twenty, dragged the thief by the shirt collar to Queen's Wharf and tied a rope around his waist. Then they dunked him in the cold November water, one dunk for every night of crime they had experienced in St. Eleanor's for the past year.

When they finally let the thief go, he and half a dozen of his cronies cleared out of town so fast, one would think they'd had a close encounter with a hornet's nest.

After that night, St. Eleanor's returned to its peaceful and crime-free way of life. Criminals wanted nothing more to do with the St. Eleanor brand of Island justice.

WILLIAM WEIR, DESERTER

William Weir was a private in the 62nd Regiment stationed in Halifax, Nova Scotia. The army had drummed him into service from the London streets when he was just fifteen. Now, at eighteen, he had had enough of military life, and on April 15, 1819, shrouded in early morning fog, he deserted his regiment. His plan was to walk his way to the United States.

He was on the Cobequid Road bound for Truro when he fell in with John Dinan, a peddler.

John Dinan was a strong man, all beef to the heels, and jolly, with a face full of sunshine. The pace Dinan set was brisk, as though his feet kept time to his constant friendly chatter. William Weir had all he could do to keep up.

They spent the night in Stewiack. Dinan shared his bed with the soldier. The following day, April 17, they were nine miles from

Truro when Weir attacked Dinan with a bayonet. He stabbed the big man several times, but Dinan stood strong. With arms hardened from years of backpacking between Truro and Halifax, Dinan threw the soldier to the ground. Then Dinan grabbed Weir by the scruff of his neck and shook him unconscious.

Despite his wounds, Dinan carried Weir and his own peddler's pack to Truro, and deposited the soldier on the sheriff's doorstep.

Weir confessed that he had planned to kill Dinan the moment they met, and that he intended to disfigure the peddler's face and dress him in his military uniform.

The jolly peddler laughed at this, and dug into his pack to hand Weir a Bible. He advised the soldier to read it before travelling the last leg of his journey—to the gallows.

CONVICTS FOR SALE

Captain John Napier contracted to transport a shipload of New Brunswick convicts to the steamy, malaria-infected island of Bermuda. On August 2, 1787, he sailed out of Saint John Harbour and across the Bay of Fundy, with the convicts below deck clapped in irons. Bermuda was the furthest thing from his mind.

At Tusket, Nova Scotia, Napier dropped anchor. In a waterfront tavern, he bargained with several Tusket merchants. He sold them seven convicts for hard cash.

Then he sailed for Shelburne, where he made a similar deal with merchants there. Shelburne officials got wind of Napier's dealings when two criminals escaped their new masters and robbed a nearby farm. The officials confronted Napier and threatened him with arrest.

Captain Napier offered to pay for the recapture of the convicts and gave his word to James Bruce, the customs collector, that he would take the convicts to Bermuda. No sooner had James Bruce turned his back than Napier was hauling sail for the open sea.

James Bruce boarded a merchant ship in the harbour, a clean-running sloop as fast as split, and ordered its captain to give chase. It sailed past the beacon at Sandy Point, past Crane Point and Roseway Beach, until it came abreast Napier's ship at Fox Rock. The merchant ship fired a cannon across Napier's bow, forcing the fugitive ship to hove to and surrender.

Two weeks later, Captain John Napier found himself back aboard his ship and sailing to Bermuda. It seems the Supreme Court had quashed the charges against Captain Napier, explaining that Napier could not be blamed for the prisoners taking "leg bail" in both Tusket and Shelburne. "Leg bail" meant the prisoners had escaped and run away. For whatever reason, the court made no mention of Napier selling the convicts as servants.

BAYARD TREASURE

In the 1780s, Colonel Samuel Bayard lived in a rambling house on the Old French Road about four miles from Middleton, Nova Scotia. His family occupied the back rooms of the house, while the front rooms served as an eighteenth-century gambling casino.

Military officers from Annapolis Royal and Halifax kept the cards playing and the dice hot both day and night. Members of the upper class in Halifax sometimes travelled the hundred or so miles to gamble. Frances Wentworth, the wife of John Wentworth who would later become governor of Nova Scotia, was one.

Jewellery, money, trinkets, property deeds, even family heirlooms changed hands on the turn of a card. And over the years, Colonel Bayard made a fortune.

All of a sudden, in 1801, when the Colonel was getting on in years, he had a change of heart brought on by a Methodist preacher named Joshua Marsden. Bayard's ill-gotten fortune troubled him. It posed an obstacle to his entering the gates of heaven.

"You must dispose of your riches," the preacher advised, "if you are to enter the Kingdom of God."

The colonel considered this divine proposition and tried taking it to heart, but could not quite bring himself to go the whole hog. He appreciated the upside of everlasting life, but the downside of giving away all his wealth was not a prospect he could cotton to. He settled on a compromise.

On a muggy summer morning in 1802, Colonel Bayard sent several hired hands and a team of horses to the granite fields at nearby Nictaux. They returned the next day with an incredibly large boulder.

Meanwhile, Bayard had secretly buried his fortune of gold and jewels in a back field, and with block and tackle and half a dozen horses, the colonel had the boulder set over top.

Whether Colonel Bayard made it through the pearly gates is a matter for religious conjecture. And whether his treasure is still buried beneath the granite boulder on the Old French Road is subject for local legend.

FATAL BOXING MATCH

John Blakney had reluctantly agreed to a five-shilling boxing match with Adam Baxendine. All he had to do to win was stay alive.

John Blakney was an eighteen-year-old private in the 20th Regiment in Halifax, a farm boy pressed into military service against his will. On July 3, 1791, Blakney's commanding officer ordered him to fight Adam Baxendine in a boxing match that night. Blakney had no choice but to agree.

Blakney knew he would be fighting for his life. Adam Baxendine was the odds-on favourite, an experienced bare-knuckles boxer whose bulldog face had the scars to prove it.

The fight was held in the North Barracks, where soldiers pushed aside bunks and furniture to make room. Pails of rum passed from hand to hand. Even the two fighters guzzled themselves painless.

There was no bell, no rounds, and no rules in this bare-knuckles match. Within minutes, young Blakney's face was bloody and raw. One eye had already swollen shut. Still Baxendine pounded him, viciously, without stop.

The soldiers hollered for blood and threw money at Baxendine's feet to encourage him to close in for the kill.

Suddenly Blakney was so terrified that he punched wildly, with all the strength he had left. His fist caught Baxendine fully on the right side of the head. The big man went down—and never got up.

With one punch, Blakney had killed Adam Baxendine. Blakney was tried the following week for murder, but his commanding officer spoke in his defence.

"After all," the officer testified, "it was only a boxing match."

The court ruled in Blakney's favour, reduced the charge to manslaughter, and sentenced the boy to a whipping.

JOHN MORLEY'S DEATH

Travelling between Halifax and Annapolis Royal in 1799, John Morley, a wealthy Halifax merchant, stopped at Dinard's Rest, an inn near the village of Middleton. He had planned to spend only the night, but ended up staying six days. He had fallen in love with the innkeeper's daughter, Marie Dinard.

Marie was a young Acadian beauty who had young men for miles fighting for her attention. A month before, Jean Torre had shot a man in a duel over her. There had been other duels as well. It was said Marie Dinard was a flirt and schemer who often played one man off against another.

John Morley promised to marry her upon his return from Annapolis Royal, where he had business to complete. He promised to prove his worth by showing her just how wealthy he was. Less than a week later, Morley returned to Dinard's Rest expecting to be married.

On October 3, 1799, Dinard's Rest was strangely quiet when a mail rider from Halifax arrived. The barn was empty of livestock, the ashes cold on the grate. Dirty dinner dishes were still on the table, and John Morley lay dead on the kitchen floor. His pockets had been turned inside out, his money purse was empty, and his gold watch was missing.

The mail rider went for the authorities. When he and the

sheriff returned, they found Dinard's Rest engulfed in flames with Morley's body still inside.

John Morley had been murdered for his money, most likely by the innkeeper, his beautiful daughter, Marie Dinard, and her outraged lover, Jean Torre. But the truth will not be known, because all three disappeared that day in 1799 and were never seen again.

MRS. DUNBAR

February 5, 1826. After receiving her application for charity, William Temple, a member of Halifax's Poor Man's Friend Society, visited Mrs. MacDonald at her home in Poplar Grove, a ramshackle neighbourhood in what was then a suburb of Halifax. The society sought impoverished but decent, God-fearing men and women for their charitable rolls. Temple found Mrs. MacDonald and her three children huddled together in a filthy room that was empty of furniture and cold enough to freeze the milk in a cow's udder. He was suitably shocked at their living conditions and included Mrs. MacDonald's name on his list.

The following day, at a society meeting, Temple described Poplar Grove as a most deplorable sight, and the home of Mrs. MacDonald particularly so. Society members sadly shook their heads at the details of Mrs. MacDonald's plight, and Henry Cogswell wanted to see for himself.

On Sunday, Cogswell found the family in a room as wretched as Temple had described, perhaps even doubly so, since Mrs. MacDonald now pulled the youngest of the three children to suckle.

However, Cogswell noticed something peculiar in the young child's behaviour—how the child withdrew from its mother and turned its head from the pap. This aroused his suspicion. He questioned the neighbours, and learned that Mrs. MacDonald had hired the children to pretend to be her own, and had promised to pay the real mothers with food she expected to glean from the Poor Man's Friend Society. Temple reported the deceit to the society and to the police.

A constable went to Poplar Grove, knocked at the appropriate door, and was greeted by a woman named Mrs. Graham, who informed the constable that Mrs. MacDonald had moved from the premises during the night. The constable reported this to Cogswell and Temple, who suspected what was about.

They returned with the constable to Poplar Grove and discovered that Mrs. Graham was indeed Mrs. MacDonald, and that Mrs. MacDonald was actually Mrs. Dunbar, a soldier's wife who had been thrown out of the barracks for her "improper conduct." When the constable reached for her arm to arrest her, Mrs. Dunbar flew into a rage and viciously scratched his face. Temple and Cogswell rushed from the house, calling for help. Two burly men arrived and, along with the constable, managed to bring the wild woman under control.

At her trial, Mrs. Dunbar pleaded for mercy and promised to amend her notorious ways. The judge took note of her wobbly legs, slurred speech, and distinct aroma of rum. He denied her request and committed her to the workhouse.

"I know the way," Mrs. Dunbar said to the judge. "I been there before."

Indeed she had. Less than two weeks previous, Mrs. Dunbar had been released from the workhouse after serving her time—for petty theft.

ROBBING THE DEAD

The schooner *Mary* sailed out of Halifax in December 1817, bound for Pictou. It carried cargo and passengers. Captain Hadley made this trip at least twice a month, and so knew these treacherous waters as well as anyone—perhaps too well, because the night the *Mary* sailed around Cape Breton Island, he was fast asleep in his bunk.

The *Mary* struck Black Rock Point near Louisbourg, and within minutes, Captain Hadley was dead, along with all the passengers and most of the crew. Two sailors survived that wreck to tell about the explosion of wood as the schooner split bow to stern when it crushed over a submerged rock. And they told about the sudden rush of water, and the screams and howls from the passengers, and the deep-throated slurp as the ship sank so quickly beneath the waves.

But the real horror was what followed. With the incoming tide, bodies and wreckage washed up on the beach. All that day and the day after, people living along that coast scavenged the beach and plundered the dead of all that was valuable. They stripped bloated bodies of clothing and jewellery, and left them naked and unburied on the beach.

When Major General Ainslie heard of such desecration, he sent a party of soldiers from Sydney to bury the dead, and issued orders for the soldiers to shoot on sight anyone caught plundering the bodies. He then went door to door among those living on the coast and searched their homes for plunder. He arrested several, and promised them a speedy trial and a certain sentence of execution.

SALL ROSS

Sall Ross was a sneak thief and highway robber who had accumulated more than twenty years of prison sentences, of which she served all of three days.

Her court record begins in May 1825. Sall was in a Halifax court for stealing jewellery from Mr. Carrit's house. Her voice was soft and low, her face pasty and sunken, her body about as thin as a length of tarred rope. The jury found her guilty and the judge sentenced her to three years in the house of correction, but deferred her time in prison until she was in better health.

No sooner was Sall Ross out the side door of the courthouse than her health improved remarkably. She went straight to Sherlock's Tavern on the waterfront and spent the next few days sinning against the eighth commandment.

Three months later, Sall was back in court, this time for breaking into Charles Loveland's store while Loveland and his wife were in the back parlour having a tea party. Once again Sall played the judge for a fool, standing before the bar with her dress stuffed with straw to give the appearance of being full with child and near to term.

The judge shook his head, pitying the pregnant thief, and again deferred her sentence, saying it would be inhumane to detain her. He paid no attention to the snickering among the spectators and the broad grin breaking over Sall Ross's face.

Six months later she was again in court. Same charge, theft; same results. This time Sall was suckling twins—not her own.

By December 1826, the courts had wised up to Sall Ross. For breaking into Hague's Dry Goods Store, she was sentenced to seven years. No compassion this time for her frail, pasty appearance. The sentence stuck.

However, Sall did only three days, then broke jail. Her last known whereabouts was the Cobequid Road. Some say she was on her way to Saint John to test the compassion of New Brunswick judges.

CAPTAIN JOHN PUTNAM

In March 1825, Captain John Putnam sailed from Boston to Liverpool, Nova Scotia, and then caught a wagon ride to Halifax along the South Shore road. On the seat beside him was a carpet bag full of one- and two-pound Nova Scotia provincial notes.

Putnam had rehearsed his lines. He told whomever he met that he had been a military officer during the War of 1812 and now sold general merchandise throughout New England.

The Halifax firm of Leonard and Greenwood on Water Street believed every word. And over brandy one evening, Leonard and Greenwood sold Putnam a shipload of goods, for which Putnam paid in cash with one- and two-pound notes—six hundred of them.

It was not until after the ship was loaded and waiting for the outgoing tide that Greenwood noticed the counterfeit. Nova Scotia provincial notes had three white bars across the bill; Putnam's had four.

Greenwood immediately went to the authorities, and the sheriff moved fast to prevent the ship from sailing. Putnam was not on board. A search of the town—the taverns, grog shops, brothels, all known haunts of the criminal class—turned up empty as well. Putnam was nowhere to be found.

Three days later, Bill Lawson, a merchant who had an eager eye for the ladies, noticed a bold swagger to one woman's walk. He followed her to Mrs. Brown's Boarding House, and played peeping Tom from the alley. The woman removed her wig. It was Putnam.

When confronted by the sheriff and Bill Lawson, Putnam drew a bayonet from under his petticoat and held off Lawson and the sheriff to make his escape out the back door. He swung from the porch and ran past the outhouse and around the coach house, but, unaccustomed to the constraints of a female girdle, failed to clear a neighbouring hedgerow. He had thorns top to bottom and betwixt and between, and that night in his jail cell, Captain John Putnam preferred standing to any other posture.

While he was in jail awaiting trial, the evidence against Putnam was mounting. On April 2, 1825, the *Novascotian* newspaper reported that Putnam had passed £250 of forged money in Liverpool, and that one of his victims had been a widow who had exchanged a pouch of gold for a £20 counterfeit note.

Then on March 26, the jail keeper, John Fielding, learned from an inside source that Putnam was planning to escape. Putnam had been buying padlocks from an outside supplier and using some of his ill-gotten money to pay for them. Because locks and locksmiths were not as sophisticated in 1825 as they are today, one skeleton key often fit several different locks. Putnam was amassing a supply of keys that he intended to use to open the padlock on his jail cell and the padlock on a door leading to the roof of the jailhouse.

Fielding put a sudden end to Putnam's plan. The jail keeper barged into Putnam's cell and found nearly a dozen keys and padlocks under the prisoner's straw tick. When he searched Putnam's person, Fielding removed a length of cod line from the sleeve of

Putnam's greatcoat. The line had been worked into a ladder, clearly for climbing down from the roof.

At his trial on April 20, Putnam confessed, adopting the usual prisoner lament that he had been down on his luck and did not think twice about taking the job offered by John Scobie, a Boston forger. According to Putnam, Scobie claimed he had easily passed counterfeit Nova Scotia Treasury notes several times before. The notes were a well-crafted counterfeit. Even the commissioner responsible for signing Nova Scotia Treasury notes testified that he would probably have accepted one himself.

The jury believed Putnam's story and convicted him of "uttering and publishing" forged notes, and not of counterfeiting. That brought a sigh of relief from Putnam. Counterfeiting was a treasonable offence and brought a sentence of execution. Uttering and publishing forged notes was a misdemeanour.

At the sentencing, Judge Haliburton stated that Putnam's crime was not against one individual, but against the entire community. He sentenced John Putnam to one year in prison, to stand one hour in the pillory, and to have one ear cut off.